LANGUAGE AND LIFE IN THE U.S.A.

LANGUAGE
AND LIFE
IN THE U.S.A.

THIRD EDITION

Volume II: Reading English

GLADYS G. DOTY
University of Colorado

JANET ROSS
Ball State University

HARPER & ROW, PUBLISHERS
New York   Evanston   San Francisco   London

LANGUAGE AND LIFE IN THE U.S.A., Third Edition
Volume II: Reading English

Standard Book Number: 06-041688-2

Library of Congress Catalog Card Number: 72-9054

CONTENTS

KEY TO ABBREVIATIONS OF THE UNITED STATES

Alabama — Ala.
Alaska — Alaska
Arizona — Ariz.
Arkansas — Ark.
California — Calif.
Colorado — Colo.
Connecticut — Conn.
Delaware — Del.
Florida — Fla.
Georgia — Ga.
Hawaii — Hawaii
Idaho — Idaho
Illinois — Ill.
Indiana — Ind.
Iowa — Iowa
Kansas — Kan.
Kentucky — Ky.
Louisiana — La.
Maine — Me.
Maryland — Md.
Massachusetts — Mass.
Michigan — Mich.
Minnesota — Minn.
Mississippi — Miss.
Missouri — Mo.

Montana — Mont.
Nebraska — Nebr.
Nevada — Nev.
New Hampshire — N.H.
New Jersey — N.J.
New Mexico — N.M.
New York — N.Y.
North Carolina — N.C.
North Dakota — N.D.
Ohio — Ohio
Oklahoma — Okla.
Oregon — Ore.
Pennsylvania — Pa.
Rhode Island — R.I.
South Carolina — S.C.
South Dakota — S.D.
Tennessee — Tenn.
Texas — Tex.
Utah — Utah
Vermont — Vt.
Virginia — Va.
Washington — Wash.
West Virginia — W. Va.
Wisconsin — Wis.
Wyoming — Wyo.

PREFACE

In the third edition of *Language and Life in the U.S.A.*, Volume II: *Reading English* has been bound separately for use in classes where reading skill is a primary goal or where reading is used as a basis and model for writing. The volume contains most of the reading selections and exercises from the previous editions, with facts, figures, and illustrations updated to fit the contemporary scene. The final essay on American English as a reflection of life in the United States has been added. As in the previous editions, the subjects of the reading selections aim not so much to acquaint students with "the great American dream" as to give a better understanding of some aspects of life in the United States today beyond the campus scene. Not included in these essays are discussions of such topics as literature, art, music, or architecture. Each of these topics is so broad that it was considered better to omit them than to deal with them only superficially. It is recommended that students read about these subjects on their own.

Reading skill depends upon a knowledge of how words are used, the perception of sentence structure patterns, and the ability to follow the organization of an essay as a whole. The vocabulary drills in *Reading English* are designed not just to increase the number of words a student knows but to teach some of the principles of English word formation, to show how meaning depends on context, and to illustrate some of the unusual or idiomatic uses of common words. Exercises on grammatical structure are aimed to help students grasp the meaning of a sentence quickly by noting the structural devices that show relationships. Other exercises help the student follow the author's organization and pick out the key devices that indicate it. Then the organizational pattern is studied in detail and the student is given an opportunity to follow it in a paragraph or composition of his own. As a student masters vocabulary and learns to perceive grammatical and rhetorical structure quickly, reading speed may be increased. As a measure, the number of words in each essay is indicated so that the instructor may time students if he wishes.

In preparing the readings on life in the U.S.A. which comprise this volume, thanks again go to those who have contributed ideas. We are particularly indebted to Dr. Rollin B. Posey, former editor at Row, Peterson & Company and Professor of Political Science at Northwestern University, for material in the essays on the Constitution, political parties, and American sports. Mrs. Orpha LeGro Haxby of Rapid City, South Dakota, kindly gave us permission to use her letter which makes up the essay *Covered Wagon Days*. From the questions asked by our students from abroad have grown the subjects for these essays and the selection of many of the details that are included. We appreciate their stimulating curiosity about America and American life.

GLADYS G. DOTY
JANET ROSS

1973
Boulder, Colorado

LANGUAGE AND LIFE IN THE U.S.A.

HOW TO READ A FOREIGN LANGUAGE

A student's ultimate aim in reading a foreign language is to be able to grasp ideas as quickly and easily as he would if he were reading his native language. Yet in early stages of language learning the first inclination of most students is to translate. Translation is a slow, laborious process. The thread of the idea may become lost, as well as the enjoyment of reading. Furthermore, an exact translation is an art in itself and not a practical procedure for everyday reading. The student should try to develop a feeling for the foreign language so that he is really *reading*, not deciphering word for word.

There are two different methods of reading a foreign language that are helpful in developing this feeling. One is a slow, careful reading to note the structure of the language and how words are used, so that one can in turn use the constructions, words, and phrases in sentences of his own. This type of *intensive* reading is practiced in Volume I. There you were aided by hearing the selections as well as by reading them. Then in conversations and written work you were asked to imitate the sentence patterns and use the vocabulary you encountered in the reading.

This method of intensive reading is very useful in mastering the basic principles of a language and in learning to use peculiarities of idiom. However, the techniques employed in this process are not those of rapid, fluent reading. To develop the ability to read rapidly and easily, you need to use a second method—*extensive* reading. This is rapid reading of a great deal of easy material. Your primary purpose here is not to learn new structures and vocabulary to the point where you can reproduce them in written and oral work of your own, but to understand the ideas being communicated as quickly and completely as possible. In reading your own language you understand more difficult words and sentence structure than you yourself use. This is true in a foreign language as well. The materials in Volume II are designed to help you develop skill in extensive reading and to give you information on aspects of American life about which foreign students often ask questions.

The main barriers to fluent reading in a foreign language are vocabulary and sentence structure. To help you overcome these barriers, the materials in this section are graded. It is assumed that you already have a basic vocabulary of some three thousand words and know something of the structure of the language. Less commonly used words are introduced gradually and are repeated. Sentence structure gradually increases in complexity throughout the readings.

1

Mastering vocabulary is not difficult at this stage. An English–native-language dictionary is an aid, but do not rely on it too heavily or you will be translating. The exact counterpart of a word in another language is difficult to find. You should have a good dictionary of the English language such as *The American College Dictionary* or *Webster's Seventh New Collegiate Dictionary.* However, when you are reading, try to look up as few words as possible. Consulting a dictionary interrupts your thought. You may be able to get the meaning of a word from its context, its use in the sentence. Notice how it is used in relation to the idea as a whole. Notice similarities to other words that you know. The reading selections are accompanied by vocabulary drills on word families, common roots, and structural forms.

Mastering structural difficulties is more of a problem. The patterns that you have learned in your intensive reading will aid you. You may have to reread portions of the selection, however, to perceive the relationship of the words to each other. Mark difficult spots, but do not spend too much time on them in an initial reading of the material. Do not lose the meaning of the selection as a whole. After you have read a larger part of the selection, the meaning of the difficult passage may become clear. Then reread the selection until you can read the difficult passages easily.

In your early stages of reading for fluency, then, the following steps are useful.

1. *Read the selection through* as rapidly as possible to *get the meaning as a whole.* Knowing the whole idea will help you to understand difficult details. Mark difficult words and difficult passages, but do not look up any more words in your dictionary than you absolutely have to. Do not spend so much time trying to unravel difficult passages that you lose the thread of the idea.

2. *Go back over the parts you have marked as difficult.* You may find that you know the meaning of many of the words from their use in the sentences, and many of the difficult passages will become clear when you see their relationship to the whole.

3. *Reread the entire selection* to fix in your mind any words and constructions that you had difficulty with the first time and to get the feeling of reading and thinking in the foreign language. Try to read the material as rapidly as possible, in the same way that you would read your native language. *Do not translate.*

If you still find words during this rereading that you must look up, it may be helpful to write them down in a notebook kept for that purpose. Words are learned most easily, however, through actual use. Reading them in context several times is usually more efficient than trying to memorize lists. Structural difficulties may take more than one rereading to fix the pattern in mind. Practice on these will make similar constructions easier when you encounter them later on. In order to improve reading speed, develop fluency, and get rid of the habit of translation or word-by-word reading, time yourself on reading of easy material or of material in which you have mastered the difficulties. Try to increase your reading speed. To aid you in computing your reading speed on the selections in this section, the number of words is given at the end of each reading.

There are certain techniques for efficient reading that apply whether you are reading your native language or any other. Though they will be more difficult to apply in reading a foreign language, they will help you develop reading skill. Some of them are:

1. *Read for ideas, not words.* Although saying the word aloud or to yourself is useful in intensive reading, it prevents reading fluency. By all means, say the unfamiliar word when you go back over the material to study vocabulary, but not when you are reading to grasp ideas quickly.

2. To read for ideas, *follow the author's organization.* Try to get the relationship between his ideas. This is particularly important in reading factual material, where you do not have the progress of a story to guide you.

3. Be flexible. *Vary your procedure to suit your purpose.* Sometimes you need to skim rapidly for general content, and sometimes you need to read slowly and carefully.

Reading for ideas by determining the general plan of the material and looking for the sequence of thought will help you in overcoming word-by-word reading. This may take time and practice, however. The focus should be on the trend of the idea that you are trying to follow, rather than on the words that make it up.

Following the author's organization helps you in reading for ideas. If you know where you are going, meaning can be determined more quickly. You can predict to a certain degree what topics the author will discuss next. Narrative is usually organized chronologically—by time sequence. Factual material may be organized this way also, but two other common types of organization are by division of ideas or by logical sequence of thought. Less often used is spatial order, sometimes used in description or exposition.

If material is organized chronologically, the development of the thought is not difficult to follow. In narrative, the progress of events aids you in following the author's ideas. In factual material, it often helps to look first for the general idea or thesis that is being developed. This is usually stated in a thesis sentence in the opening paragraph. Each following paragraph, or group of paragraphs, will develop some aspect of this central idea and will have a topic sentence in which this particular aspect is stated. Sometimes the idea of a main division is not stated in a topic sentence, but is implied. You can get the general trend of the selection by looking for these main ideas. In skimming, or making a quick survey of material to see what it contains, this is the technique used. Key words often serve as guideposts to help you follow the development of the author's thought. In material that is organized chronologically, look for such words as *first, next, then, after that, finally, at last, the following year.* These usually introduce the main ideas. The general development of Essay 6, "A Story of the West," is indicated by such words as *finally, later,* and *all went well until.*

If material is organized by division of ideas, you expect to find the ideas listed. If the author is discussing government, he might use such divisions as legislative, executive, and judicial branches. If he talks of religion, he might speak of Christianity, Buddhism, and Mohammedanism. If he is explaining the reasons for the defeat of the South in the American Civil War, he might mention the northern blockade of southern ports, the lack of industrialization in the South, and the breaking of lines of communication.

The essay you are reading now has two main divisions: (1) methods of reading a foreign language and (2) general methods of improving reading. Each of these main divisions of thought is, in turn, developed by further division. The methods of reading a foreign language are (a) intensive and (b) extensive. General methods of improving reading are (a) avoiding word-by-word reading, (b) following the author's organization, and (c) varying reading procedure to suit purpose. Certain key words, generally found near the beginning of a paragraph, help to make the reader aware of the author's division of thought. The first paragraph of this essay is introductory. The first sentence of the second paragraph contains the key words "two different methods" to guide the reader. In the next sentence the words "One is . . ." point to the first division. In the third paragraph is the transitional sentence beginning, "However, the techniques employed in this process are not . . . ." This leads to a discussion of the second method. In the next sentence the key words "a second method" point it out. Common key words to indicate organization by division are *first of all, second, a second reason, also, in addition, furthermore.*

In the method of organization by logical sequence of ideas the stages of the author's thinking are traced. This type of organization is used in presenting a problem and solution or cause and effect. Order of the ideas is fixed because each idea develops logically from a previous one. Key words often used in organization by logical sequence of ideas are *therefore, as a result, the reason for this, the cause of this,* and similar expressions. Words that indicate contrast in thought are *however, but, on the other hand, in spite of this, nevertheless.* Often there is a summary at the end, which is useful in skimming or in getting a general idea of the content. Look for such words as *in conclusion, in summary*, and *as we have seen*. In material organized by logical sequence of ideas, the main idea is often stated at the end rather than at the beginning. It is a conclusion drawn from the reasoning of the article.

A third technique for efficient reading in your own or a foreign language is to be flexible. Vary the way you read to suit your purpose. Sometimes you want to skim an article quickly to see whether it contains material you will find useful. Sometimes a slow, careful reading is necessary to grasp the ideas. Sometimes you want to read critically to analyze the validity of what the author is saying. You ask: Is his argument logical? Does he give sufficient supporting evidence? What is the tone of the selection? At other times you want to read solely for enjoyment. How you read depends also upon the difficulty of the material and your familiarity with the subject.

The articles in this section are designed to help you speed up your reading of the type of material that you will find in textbooks. They deal for the most part with factual material and are read more slowly than fiction. To learn to read a foreign language rapidly, to read for ideas, to learn vocabulary, and to get used to sentence structure, the additional reading of fiction is a great help and is strongly urged. One Polish student says he taught himself English by reading murder mysteries and going to American movies. Of the mystery stories he says, "There was enough action on every page to make me keep reading." Other students have learned from reading newspapers, stories written for young readers, and elementary and junior high school textbooks in their special field of study. Such textbooks give the student the advantage of being able to anticipate ideas and help him learn the special vocabulary of his field.

The mastery of all the techniques of reading a foreign language is a long-term goal. It takes constant practice to learn to read another language as you would your own.

GETTING ALONG IN AMERICA

Word Study

At the beginning of each reading selection in Volume II there is a list of less common words that will be encountered in the selection. Study the meanings. Note principles which you are asked to remember in order to discover meanings for yourself.

Compare the parts of a new word (root, prefix, or suffix) with similar parts of other words you already know.

Look at the sentence in which a word occurs (linguistic context) and guess what function the word serves in the sentence.

Keep in mind what has been said previously in the selection that you are reading (the semantic context), and guess from the situation what the word may mean.

Be aware that a given word may have more than one meaning, and that it is the reader's responsibility to recognize the particular meaning in a given sentence.

Here are the words to study before you read the following selection. Learn the meaning and the pronunciation of each before you start reading.

1. temperamental /tɛmprəméntəl/
2. generalization /dʒɛnrələzéʃən/
3. characteristic /kɛrɛktərístɪk/
4. acquaintance /əkwéntəns/
5. receptionist /rɪsépʃənɪst/
6. customary /kɔ́stəmɛrɪ/
7. proverb /prɑ́vərb/
8. tip /tɪ́p/
9. status /stétəs/
10. compliment /kɑ́mpləmənt/
11. ridiculous /rɪdíkyələs/
12. obvious /ɑ́bvɪəs/
13. consistent /kənsístənt/
14. embarrassment /ɛmbɛ́rəsmənt/
15. confuse /kənfyúz/

Word related to words you may already know:

	Related words	Common prefix or suffix
1. *temperamental*	temper, temperament	-al adjective ending
2. *generalization*	general, generalize	-ation noun ending

3. *characteristic*	character	*-istic* adjective or noun ending
4. *acquaintance*	acquaint	*-ance* noun ending
5. *receptionist*	reception, receive	*-ist* noun ending indicating person
6. *customary*	custom, accustom	*-ary* adjective ending

Words whose meaning can be determined by context:

7. *proverb* "When in Rome, do as the Romans do." This is an old *proverb*.
8. *tip* You are expected to give a *tip*, or small amount of money, as a sign of appreciation to an employee of a hotel or restaurant who performs services for you.

Words that may need definition:

9. *status* condition, position, or standing (socially, politically, legally, or otherwise) (His *status* as an American citizen has not been determined.)
10. *compliment* something said to praise a person (The employer gave the employee a *compliment* on his work.)
11. *ridiculous* condition of being clearly untrue or unreasonable, absurd or laughable (This is a *ridiculous* situation; I have no money to pay for my dinner because I left it all at home.)
12. *obvious* easy to see or understand (When you have lost something, you may find it in an *obvious* place.)
13. *consistent* repeated in uniform fashion (There is no *consistent* practice regarding tipping in the United States.)
14. *embarrassment* the state of not being at ease, or of feeling inadequate (When he discovered he had mistaken the young lady for someone else, the young man suffered great *embarrassment*.)
15. *confuse* to perplex or bewilder (Foreign students are likely to be *confused* by some of the customs in the United States.)

Reading Suggestions

To develop skill in reading English, read the essay through as quickly as you can, not stopping to look up words in the dictionary. Focus attention on the overall progression of thought rather than interrupting it when you encounter a difficult word. Learn to tolerate a little ambiguity as a normal part of learning to read in a foreign language. After you have read the selection once, read it again, marking difficult passages. Then study the words and structures in these passages and reread the passage until you can read it as quickly as you read the easier parts. After doing the exercises at the end of the selection, if you still do not understand passages containing certain words or constructions, bring your problem to class for explanation.

GETTING ALONG IN AMERICA

1. "When in Rome, do as the Romans do." So goes an old English *proverb* (7). This is generally good advice for a person in a strange country. In order to follow it, it is necessary to know what the Romans do and, more important, what their attitudes and beliefs are.

2. Every society has its own peculiar customs and ways of acting. The United States contains over 180 million people. They have a wide variety of national backgrounds, so there are bound to be regional and *temperamental* (1) differences. *Generalizations* (2) about American manners and customs are difficult to make, particularly in a society that is changing as rapidly as that of present-day America. The reader should remember that when he reads that Americans do this or that or think this or that, not all Americans do or think this particular thing, or if they do today, they may not tomorrow. There are exceptions. In the following pages, however, the authors attempt to point out a few *characteristics* (3) of behavior that are common enough to make generalizations about. These may help you to understand American society and get along in it more easily. Later essays will deal with the even more difficult question of beliefs and attitudes. In these essays students should not misinterpret the use of the term *American* as applied to the people of the United States to mean that these Americans think that they are the only people living in the Western hemisphere. The name *United States of America* is often shortened to *America* and thus the people are *Americans.* The nature of the language also fosters use of the term. One cannot say "United Statesman," as "statesman" has a different meaning, and "United Statesian" would be cumbersome.

INTRODUCTIONS AND GREETINGS

3. Except on official occasions such as formal receptions for distinguished guests, American society has a certain amount of informality. This informality is seen in customs of introductions and greetings. On most occasions one need not be particularly conscious of social *status* (9). Americans generally ignore it. In spite of the informality, however, there are rules of good manners and social patterns that are followed.

4. There are rules for introducing people to each other. A younger person is generally introduced to an older one, a man is introduced to a woman, a guest to the host or hostess, and a person to the group. For instance, one would say, "Mrs. Gray, this is my younger sister Janet." Or "Margaret, may I present Mr. Bradley?" And then one adds, "Mr. Bradley, this is my friend Margaret Hoskins from Chicago." One could phrase the introduction like this: "Miss Hoskins, I would like to introduce Mr. Bradley," or "Miss Hoskins, do you

know Mr. Bradley?" One must be sure that each one knows the family name of the other. The usual reply to an introduction is, "How do you do?" or "How do you do? I'm pleased to meet you." Adding the name of the person just introduced is also common: "How do you do, Mr. Bradley?"

5. In many European countries handshaking is a social courtesy whenever people meet. The custom of shaking hands in the United States varies in different parts of the country and among different groups of people. It is somewhat difficult to make a set rule. Shaking hands is more likely to be reserved for formal occasions. When men are introduced, they generally shake hands. Women shake hands less frequently. Two women who meet for the first time often do not shake hands unless one is an especially honored guest. If a man and woman are being introduced, they may or may not shake hands. Usually the woman extends her hand first. If an American does not shake hands when meeting an old acquaintance, he is not being impolite. He may be paying him the *compliment* (10) of considering him one of the group.

6. When a person meets an *acquaintance* (4) on the street, the most common form of greeting in America is "Hello." It is said on most informal occasions and often on quite formal ones. More formal greetings are "Good morning," "Good afternoon," and "Good evening." (Oddly enough, "Good night" and "Goodbye" are said only on parting.) The formal "How do you do?" is generally used when one is introduced to a stranger.

7. Quite often any greeting (except "How do you do?") is followed by the question "How are you?" Only occasionally does the questioner really want to stop and learn about your health. He simply asks the question to show friendly concern about you and to keep the "Hello" or "Good morning" from seeming too short. If a person does have time to explain how he is, he is not supposed to do so. An individual may be going through great mental or physical pain and still reply to the question "How are you?" by saying "Just fine. How are things with you?" or "Fine, thank you. Isn't it a beautiful day?" This habit can result in a rather *ridiculous* (11) situation. When a patient comes to see a doctor, the *receptionist* (5) may ask, "How are you?" The patient may reply, "Just fine," when it is quite *obvious* (12) that if this were true, he would not be at the doctor's office.

8. On parting, one says, "Good-bye. It's been nice seeing you," or "I hope to see you again soon," or something of the sort. "Good night" is a farewell used late in the evening. "Good-bye" is suitable at any time.

TIPPING

9. In many countries there is a fixed charge for personal services.

A certain percentage may be added to the bill at a hotel or restaurant "for the service." In other places the customer may be expected to give a *tip* (8), or small amount of money, as a sign of appreciation whenever services are performed. In the United States there is no *consistent* (13) practice in regard to tipping. The custom is more common in a large city than in a small town. A native American may often be in doubt about when and how much to tip when he is in a city that is strange to him. In general, however, a tip is expected by the porter who carries your baggage, by taxi drivers (except, perhaps, in small towns), and by those who serve you in hotels and restaurants.

10. When you pick up your incoming luggage at an airport, you may tip the man who takes it to the taxi or airport limousine. He usually expects 35 cents a bag for his service. In some cities the taxi that takes you to your hotel may have one meter that registers the cost of the trip and another that shows a fixed charge, usually about 20 cents, for "extras." In some cities the taxi driver may expect a tip in addition to the "extra," especially if he carries your suitcase. If no "extra" is charged, a tip is usually given. Hotels generally do not make a service charge, though there are places where one is added. It is *customary* (6), however, to give something to the porter who carries your suitcases and shows you to your room. In case of doubt, 35 cents for each bag he carries is satisfactory. In a restaurant you generally leave about 15 percent of the bill in small change on that table as a tip for the person who has served you. A service charge is generally not included except in some of the larger, more expensive places. If the order is small—a cup of coffee at a lunch counter, or something of the sort—a tip is not usually expected.

11. The practice of tipping for other services is even more varied. In large cities one usually tips the shoeshine boy, the barber, or the hairdresser. Contrary to the custom in some European countries, one does not tip the usher who shows him to his seat in a theater.

DINING CUSTOMS

12. Every land has its own peculiar dining custom, and the United States is no exception. Americans feel that the first rule of being a courteous guest is to be prompt. If a person is invited to dinner at six-thirty, the hostess expects him to be there at six-thirty or not more than a few minutes after. Because she usually does her own cooking, she times the meal so that the hot rolls and the coffee and meat will be at their best at the time she asks the guest to come. If he is late, the food will not be so good, and the hostess will be disappointed. When the guest cannot come on time, he calls his host or hostess on the telephone, gives the reason, and tells at what time he thinks he can come.

13. As guests continue to arrive, the men in the group stand when

a woman enters and remain standing until she has found a chair. A man always rises when he is being introduced to a woman. A woman does not rise when she is being introduced either to a man or a woman unless the woman is much older.

14. When the guests sit down at a dinner table, it is customary for the men to help the ladies by pushing their chairs under them. Until the meal is under way, if the dinner is in a private home, a guest may avoid *embarrassment* (14) by leaving the talking to someone else. Some families have a habit of offering a prayer of thanks before they eat. Other families do not. If a prayer is offered, everyone sits quietly with bowed head until the prayer is over. If the family does not follow the custom, there is no pause in the conversation.

15. Even an American may be *confused* (15) by the number of knives, forks, and spoons beside his plate when he sits down to a formal dinner. The rule is simple, however: Use them in the order in which they lie, beginning from the outside. Or watch the hostess and do what she does. The small fork on the outside on the left is for salad, which is often served with the soup. The spoon on the outside at the right is for soup, and so on. Sometimes there is a separate little knife, called a butter spreader, on a small bread-and-butter plate at the left. As the bread is passed, each guest puts his piece on the bread-and-butter plate.

16. There is a difference between American and European customs in using the knife and fork. The European keeps the knife in the right hand, the fork in the left. He uses both hands in eating. The American, on the contrary, may use just one hand whenever possible and keep the other one on his lap. He constantly changes his fork to the left hand when he has to cut his meat. Between bites he lays his fork on his plate while drinking his coffee or buttering his bread. The European is more apt to drink his coffee after his meal and to keep his knife and fork in hand until he finishes eating.

17. Since Americans lay their silverware down a great deal during the meal, certain customs have developed. It is not considered good manners to leave a spoon in a soup bowl or coffee cup or any other dish. It is put where it will lie flat (a coffee spoon on the saucer, a soup spoon on the service plate under the soup bowl., etc.). By doing this, one is less likely to knock the silverware onto the floor or spill the food. Another difference in custom is that the American uses the side of his soup spoon, not the tip.

18. Americans do not use silverware for eating bread. They hold it in their fingers, usually breaking it first. A person is considered peculiar if he anchors a slice of bread firmly on his plate with his fork, butters the whole slice with his knife, and then cuts it up and eats it with his knife and fork, thus avoiding greasy fingers. Other things that Americans eat with their fingers are corn on the cob, celery,

radishes, and olives. In America a person does not eat lettuce that way, nor does he pick up his soup bowl to drink what remains at the bottom, even though he can get the last drop that way.

19. If for any reason a guest has to leave the table during a meal, he always asks his hostess, "Will you please excuse me for a minute?" When the meal is finished, the guests put their napkins on the table and rise, the men again helping the ladies with their chairs. Guests do not fold their napkins in the original folds unless they are house guests and intend to stay for more than one meal. The napkin of the passing guest is immediately put into the laundry.

20. Following the dinner, the guests usually stay for two or three hours, but the thoughtful person is careful not to overstay his welcome. The host and hostess may urge him to stay longer in order to be polite, but most dinner parties break up about eleven o'clock.

21. As the guests leave, it is the custom to thank the hostess for a very pleasant evening. One may say anything that truly expresses his appreciation. Common expressions are, "Goodbye. It was so nice of you to have me," or "Goodbye. It's been a thoroughly enjoyable evening," or "Thank you. I've had such a good time." For larger favors than a dinner party, such as an overnight or weekend visit, it is customary to send a thank-you note (which is called a "bread-and-butter letter"), and quite often people later send a small gift such as a box of candy or some flowers as a sign of their appreciation.
(*2296 words*)

EXERCISES

I. Comprehension of Details
Indicate whether each of the following statements is true or false by writing the letter T or F in the space provided.

_____ 1. Because of the informality of American society, there are no rules or standards of social behavior.

_____ 2. In introductions the older person is generally introduced to the younger.

_____ 3. In America handshaking is more likely to be reserved for formal occasions than in many European countries.

_____ 4. The practice of tipping is somewhat more common in small towns in America than in cities.

_____ 5. If a guest is invited to dinner at six-thirty, he is expected to arrive at that time or very soon after.

_____ 6. At a dinner party it is customary for a man to rise when a woman enters the room.

_____ 7. One should leave immediately after the dinner in a private home.

_____ 8. A house guest tries to save his hostess from having a big laundry bill.

_____ 9. A traveler does not tip as much as people who stay at home.

_____ 10. Table manners are important to educated Americans.

II. Skimming Exercise

As quickly as possible, find the number of the paragraph in which each of the following is mentioned or discussed.

1. customs in regard to using a knife
2. suggestions for showing appreciation for social courtesies
3. greetings used in a doctor's office
4. the population of the United States
5. the content of the later essays

III. Vocabulary Exercises

WORD STUDY

Fill each of the blanks in the following sentences with an appropriate word from the list at the beginning of this selection.

1. There are so many different kinds of people in America that it is difficult to make _____ about customs.
2. We all like to be praised; thus we like people who _____ us.
3. The porter did so many thoughtful things for me that I gave him a big _____.
4. When a person knows the customs of a country, he is much less likely to find a situation which causes him _____.
5. There is not absolute rule for handshaking in the United States. Practices in regard to handshaking are not _____.
6. When I went to the doctor's office, his _____ took my name and asked me to be seated until the doctor could see me.
7. I don't know him very well. My _____ with him is slight.
8. When a horse is gentle one minute and frisky the next, we say it is _____.
9. All his life he has been an honest person. It is _____ to believe that he has suddenly become a thief.
10. You are excited. It is _____ that something unusual has happened.

WORDS WITH MULTIPLE MEANINGS

Some words have more than one legitimate use and meaning. The sentences in each of the following groups illustrate a legitimate use of a given word. Which sentence illustrates the use of the word (or idiomatic or figurative expression) in the selection that you have just

read? Circle the letter that precedes the sentence. Numbers in parentheses refer to paragraphs in the essay.
1. are *bound to be* regional differences (2)
   a. The book is *bound* in leather.
   b. Children are *bound* to have some accidents as they grow up.
   c. The prisoner's hands were *bound.*
2. may be *paying* him a compliment (5)
   a. John is not *paying* attention; he is sleeping.
   b. John is not *paying* his income tax.
3. to keep the "Hello" or "Good morning" from seeming too *short* (7)
   a. The rope seems too *short.*
   b. The villain passed a *short* check.
   c. His answer was rudely *short.*
4. is a *fixed* charge (9)
   a. The mechanic *fixed* the car.
   b. He *fixed* his eyes on me.
   c. There is now a *fixed* price for wheat.
5. whenever *services* are performed (9)
   a. The Sunday church *services* are at nine and eleven o'clock.
   b. My lawyer's *services* cost a lot.
   c. Which branch of the armed *services* is Ted Smith in?
6. until the meal is *under* way (14)
   a. The house is *under* construction.
   b. The mouse ran *under* the table.
   c. *Under* the terms of the contract, he must perform these services.
7. *leaving* the talking to someone else (14)
   a. He was fined for *leaving* the scene of the accident.
   b. Children are noted for making a mess and *leaving* the cleaning up to their parents.
8. is more *apt* to drink his coffee (16)
   a. That is an *apt* remark; it exactly fits the situation.
   b. Roses are *apt* to grow wild here.

IV. Comprehension of Grammatical Structure

EXERCISE A

In the passage below supply the words that have been omitted. Do not look at the essay. When you have finished, check with paragraph 5.

1. In many European countries handshaking _____ a social courtesy whenever people _____. 2. The custom of shaking hands _____ the United States varies in different parts of the country and _____ different groups of people. 3. It _____ somewhat difficult to make a _____ rule. 4. Shaking hands is more _____

to be reserved for formal _____. 5. When men are introduced, they _____ shake hands. 6. Women shake hands _____ frequently. 7. Two women who meet _____ the first time often do _____ shake hands unless one is _____ especially honored guest. 8. If a _____ and woman are being introduced, _____ may or may not shake _____. 9. Usually the woman extends her _____ first.

EXERCISE B
After you have finished checking Exercise A with the paragraph in the essay, answer the following questions on it.

1. In sentence 1 is there any word that could be substituted structurally for *is*?
2. Could any word be substituted for *in* in sentence 2?
3. In sentence 3 what words might be substituted for *set* in "a set rule" with approximately the same meaning?
4. In sentence 4 why is the verb *is* rather than *are* used after hands? What is the subject of the sentence?
5. In sentence 5 could any word be substituted for *generally* without changing the meaning?
6. In sentence 8 why is *they* used?
7. In sentence 9 can the word *first* be placed before *extends*? Is the meaning changed?

V. Comprehension of Main Ideas and Organization Pattern

1. What aspects of American life did the authors feel needed explanation for visitors? What is the quickest clue to the answer?
2. In the section on introductions and greetings, how did the subtitle give you a clue as to the order in which those two subjects would be discussed?
3. Why is the paragraph on handshaking a good transition (bridge of thought) between the discussion of introductions and the discussion of greetings?
4. "Introductions and Greetings" is organized according to topics. Is the material in "Dining Customs" organized overall according to time or space or topics? In the latter section note transitional words at the beginnings of paragraphs such as "As guests continue to arrive," "When the guests sit down," "Following the dinner."
5. "Dining Customs" contains suggestions about what to do (a) before dinner, (b) during dinner, (c) after dinner. Is the discussion of what to do during dinner (paragraphs 14–19) organized according to time, space, or topics? Give the reason for your answer.

VI. Composition

OF INTERMEDIATE DIFFICULTY

Jim Smith is introducing his sister Eleanor, who is a biology major at the university, to his friend Bill Patterson, who is studying prelaw. Write a dialogue containing the introduction and a short bit of the conversation which would follow.

ADVANCED

Write a short paper on one of the following.
1. Forms of Greeting in My Native Country
2. Dining Customs in My Native Country

Essay 2

AMERICAN SOCIAL RELATIONS

Word Study

1. inconvenience /ɪnkənvínyəns/
2. integrity /ɪntégrɪti/
3. creditor /krédətər/
4. apology /əpálədʒi/
5. modesty /mádəsti/
6. congratulation /kəngrætʃuléʃən/
7. tuxedo /təksído/
8. employee /ɛmplɔ́ɪi/
9. flattery /flǽtəri/
10. sportsmanship /spórtsmənʃɪp/
11. competition /kɑmpətíʃən/
12. excel /ɛksél/
13. stun /stən/

Try to determine the meaning of the above words from their use in the following sentences.

1. Something that is a trouble or a bother or not easy is called an *inconvenience.*
2. Mr. Hawkins is honest. His *integrity* is unquestioned.
3. A *creditor* is a person to whom you owe money—a person who has given you credit.
4. If you have received an affront from someone, perhaps that person will give you an *apology.* He will say he is sorry.
5. A modest person does not tell you how well he can do things. He does not talk much about his many accomplishments. Some people have no *modesty.*
6. You congratulate a person when he has done something unusually well. You tell him that you are happy because of his success. You give him your *congratulations.*
7. For formal occasions in the evening, a man wears a *tuxedo*—a black dress jacket.
8. An *employee* is one who works for someone else for pay. A factory hires many employees.
9. What he said was just *flattery,* for he praised me so much that I I am sure he did not mean what he said.
10. It is good *sportsmanship* for the winner to say good things about the loser in a game. It is what a sportsman does.

18

11. In a *competition* a person tries to do better than anyone else (for example, win a race or sell more clothes).
12. He *excels* at playing tennis. He plays tennis better than anyone else.
13. That blow on the head *stunned* him. He felt dizzy. Sometimes people are stunned by surprising news. They are so surprised that their brains stop working, and they cannot think of what to say.

Reading Suggestions
Read through the following essay as quickly as possible to get the central idea or the main point that the author is trying to make about American social relations. Note carefully the first sentence of each paragraph. It will generally give you a cue as to the topic that the paragraph deals with.

AMERICAN SOCIAL RELATIONS

1. American society is much more informal than that of many other countries and, in some ways, is characterized by less social distinction. The American mixture of pride in achievement and sense of "I'm just as good as anybody else," along with lack of importance placed on personal dignity, is sometimes difficult for a foreigner to understand. Americans in general do not like to be considered inferior, and they grumble loudly about *inconveniences* (1) or not getting a "fair deal." Yet they do not make a point of their personal honor. As an illustration of the difference between European and American reactions in this respect, John Whyte in *American Words and Ways* gives the following account.

A . . . [European] professor [visiting in America] was once sent a bill for hospital services which he had never enjoyed. The bill was accompanied by a strong letter demanding payment. It was obvious that a mistake in names had been made, but the professor, thoroughly aroused by this reflection on his character and financial *integrity* (2), wrote a vigorous letter of reply (which an American might also have done). But in this letter of reply he demanded that the *creditor* (3) write him a formal letter of *apology* (4) . . . for this reflection on his honor. Since no publicity could possibly have been given to the mistake, for mistake it was, most Americans in that situation, after getting the matter off their chests (or without doing that) would have let the matter rest.[1]

2. An example of the same thing may be that although Americans

[1] John Whyte, *American Words and Ways*. New York: The Viking Press, Inc., 1943, p. 135. Reprinted by permission of the publishers.

like to talk about their accomplishments, it is their custom to show a certain *modesty* (5) in reply to compliments. When someone praises an American upon his achievement or upon his personal appearance, which, incidentally, is a very polite thing to do in America, the American turns it aside. If someone should say, *"Congratulations* (6) upon being elected president of the club," an American is expected to reply, "Well, I hope I can do a good job," or something of the sort. Or if someone says, "That's a pretty blue necktie you are wearing," an American is likely to say, "I'm glad you like it," or "Thank you. My wife gave it to me for my birthday." The response to a compliment seldom conveys the idea, "I, too, think I'm pretty good."

3. Likewise, there are fewer social conventions that show social differences in America. Students do not rise when a teacher enters the room. One does not always address a person by his title, such as "Professor" or "Doctor," in the case of a holder of a Ph.D. (Doctor of Philosophy degree). ("Doctor" is always used, however, for a doctor of medicine.) The respectful "sir" is not always used in the northern and western parts of the country.

4. Clothing in America, as in every place in the world, to a certain degree reflects a person's social position and income, or, at least among the young, his attitudes toward society or toward himself. Yet no person is restricted to a certain uniform or manner of dress because of his occupation or class in society. A bank president may wear overalls to paint his house and is not ashamed of either the job or the clothing, and a common laborer may wear a rented *tuxedo* (7) at his daughter's wedding.

5. Yet in spite of all the informality, America is not completely without customs that show consciousness of social distinction. For example, one is likely to use somewhat more formal language when talking to superiors. While the informal "Hello" is an acceptable greeting from *employee* (8) to employer, the employee is more apt to say, "Hello, Mr. Ferguson," whereas the employer may reply, "Hello, Jim." Southerners make a point of saying "Yes, sir," or "Yes, ma'am," or "No, sir," or "No, ma'am," when talking to an older person or a person in position of authority. Although this is good form all over the United States, "Yes, Mr. Weston" or "No, Mrs. Baker" is somewhat more common in a similar situation in the North or West.

6. Certain other forms of politeness are observed on social occasions. Though people wear hats less now than in the past, women still occasionally wear hats in church and at public social functions (except those that are in the evening).

7. In America there are still customs by which a man may show respect for a woman. He opens the door for her and lets her precede him through it. He walks on the side of the walk nearest the street. He takes her arm when crossing a street or descending a stairway. A

younger person also shows respect for an older one in much the same fashion, by helping the older person in things requiring physical exertion or involving possible accident.

8. American surface informality often confuses the foreigner because he interprets it to mean no formality at all. He does not understand the point at which informality stops. A teacher, though friendly, pleasant, and informal in class, expects students to study hard, and he grades each student's work critically and carefully. He also expects to be treated with respect. Although students are free to ask questions about statements made by the teacher, and may say that they disagree with what he says, they are not expected to contradict him. Similarly, in boy–girl relationships a foreign student should not mistake the easy relationship and the *flattery* (9) that are part of the dating pattern in the United States, nor presume that it means more than it does.

9. Also, because an American is perhaps more likely to admit and laugh at his own mistakes than one who stands more on his dignity, a foreigner sometimes does not know how to handle the American's apparent modesty. The American is quite ready to admit certain weaknesses, such as "I never was very good at mathematics," "I'm a rotten tennis player," or "I'm the world's worst bridge player." However, the stranger must not be too quick to agree with him. Americans think it is all right, even sporting, to admit a defect in themselves, but they feel that it is almost an insult to have someone else agree. A part of the American idea of good *sportsmanship* (10) is the point of being generous to a loser. This attitude is carried over into matters that have nothing to do with *competition* (11). If a man talks about his weak points, the listener says something in the way of encouragement or points to other qualities in which the speaker *excels* (12). An American student reports that when he was in a foreign country he was completely *stunned* (13) when he said to a native, "I don't speak your language very well," and the native replied, "I should say you don't." In a similar situation an American would have commented, "Well, you have only been here two months," or "But you're making progress."

10. Although Americans are quite informal, it is best for a foreigner, in case of doubt, to be too formal rather than not formal enough. Consideration for others is the basis of all courtesy.

(1173 words)

EXERCISES

I. Comprehension of Details
Indicate whether each of the following statements is true or false

by writing the letter T or F in the space provided.

_____ 1. The American does not stand as much on his personal dignity as people from many other countries do.

_____ 2. Because Americans feel that they are just as good as anybody else, they rarely show modesty about their personal achievements.

_____ 3. In the United States it is polite to compliment someone on his clothing.

_____ 4. America is completely without customs that show consciousness of social distinction.

_____ 5. A man removes his hat on any public occasion when he wants to show respect.

_____ 6. In America the informal "Hello" is appropriate on every occasion.

_____ 7. A teacher, though friendly and pleasant in an American classroom, expects to be treated with respect.

_____ 8. One does not always address an American by his title, such as "Doctor" or "Professor."

_____ 9. The friendly classroom conduct of American college instructors indicates that they are less strict in requirements.

_____ 10. Because Americans are informal, it is practically impossible for a foreigner to make a social mistake.

II. Skimming Exercise

As quickly as possible, find the number of the paragraph in which each of the following is mentioned or discussed.

1. an illustration of the differences in American and European reactions to a mistake on the part of a business office
2. American response to compliments
3. the use of titles in the United States
4. customs by which a man shows respect to a woman
5. customs that show social distinction
6. student–teacher relationships in the United States
7. an American's reaction toward his own weaknesses

III. Vocabulary Exercises

A WORD STUDY

Fill each of the blanks in the following sentences with an appropriate word from the list at the beginning of this selection

1. If a person has offended you in some way, perhaps he will give you an _____.

2. Business firms like to do business with clients of financial _____.

3. A person who talks too much about his own achievements may be said to have no _____.

4. If someone has achieved success in a certain field or won an honor of some sort, you give him your _____.
5. If you praise a person more than he feels he deserves, he may tell you that your words are _____.
6. Sometimes you agree to do something you don't want to do, even though you consider it an _____.
7. Everyone likes to _____ in some line of endeavor.
8. If two people do well in the same line of work, there may be keen _____.
9. In America accepting defeat gracefully is called good _____.
10. A person to whom you owe some money is your _____.

WORDS WITH MULTIPLE MEANINGS
Circle the letter preceding the sentence in which the italicized word is used in the same sense as it was used in the selection you have just read.
1. a bill for hospital services which he had never *enjoyed* (1)
    a. We *enjoyed* the symphony.
    b. We *enjoyed* the occasion to be with you.
    c. Since I have no musical talent, giving a concert is an experience I have never *enjoyed*.
2. aroused by this *reflection* on his character (1)
    a. I saw my *reflection* in the pool.
    b. The scholar wanted to go away to a quiet spot where he could do some *reflection*.
    c. The child's lack of manners is a *reflection* on his rearing.
3. He wrote a *vigorous* letter. (1)
    a. He did *vigorous* exercise every morning.
    b. His protest against the idea was *vigorous*.
    c. He is a *vigorous* person.
4. A younger person also shows respect for an older one in much the same *fashion*. (7)
    a. It is the *fashion* to wear your hair long.
    b. He dressed in the *fashion* of an older era.
    c. I don't understand the *fashion* in which he does this.
5. An American is more likely to *admit* his own mistakes. (9)
    a. We *admit* to the organization only those who have passed an examination.
    b. The receptionist will *admit* you to the office.
    c. Some people never *admit* that they are wrong.
6. one who *stands* on his dignity (9)
    a. I hope you will not *stand* on ceremony but will visit us often.
    b. How do you *stand* this heat?
    c. I had to *stand* and wait for the bus for an hour.

7. He does not know how to *handle* the American's apparent modesty. (9)
   a. I do not know how to *handle* this matter.
   b. *Handle* this with care.
   c. Our company does not *handle* that product.
8. I'm a *rotten* tennis player. (9)
   a. This apple is *rotten*.
   b. He did a *rotten* job on this examination.
   c. There is something *rotten* about the whole idea.

IV. Comprehension of Grammatical Structure

EXERCISE A

In which sentence in each group below does the word *that* have a different function than in the other two? The paragraph in which the sentence appears is given in parentheses.
1. a. American society is much more informal than *that* of many other countries. (1)
   b. An example of the same thing may be *that* although Americans like to talk about their achievements, it is their custom to show a certain modesty. (2)
   c. Likewise, there are fewer social conventions *that* show social differences in America. (3)
2. a. A foreign student should not mistake the easy relationship and the flattery *that* are part of the dating pattern in the United States. (8)
   b. He should not presume *that* it means more than it does. (8)
   c. They feel *that* it is almost an insult to have someone else agree. (9)

EXERCISE B

Draw vertical lines in each of the sentences below to separate the main sentence pattern and the subordinate patterns. If there is only one sentence pattern, do not mark the separation. Numbers in parentheses refer to paragraphs in the essay.

Students do not rise | when a teacher enters the room.

1. Yet in spite of all the informality, America is not completely without customs that show consciousness of social distinction. (5)
2. While the informal "Hello" is an acceptable greeting from employee to employer, the employee is more apt to say "Hello, Mr. Ferguson," whereas the employer may reply, "Hello, Jim." (5)
3. He takes her arm when crossing a street or descending a stairway. (7)

V. Comprehension of Main Ideas and Organizational Pattern

1. The author's purpose in Essay 1 was to give visitors in America information that would help them adjust to living in the United States. Do the authors have the same purpose in Essay 2?

2. Place a check mark before whichever of the following is the best statement of the main idea of this selection. Be prepared to justify your answer by referring to the structural pattern of the essay and showing why the alternatives you have not selected are inadequate.

   a. Although Americans are quite informal, it is best for a foreigner, in case of doubt, to be too formal rather than not formal enough.

   b. In spite of the informal manner in which Americans behave, America is not completely without customs that show consciousness of social distinction.

   c. American surface informality often confuses the foreigner because he interprets it to mean no formality at all.

   d. Foreigners are often confused because American surface informality may conceal underlying social consciousness.

3. The following are the principal ideas developed in "American Social Relations." In the blanks before each Roman numeral list the numbers of the paragraphs devoted to the development of each main point.

   _____   I. American society is more informal than the society of many other countries.

   _____   II. America does have some customs that reflect social distinctions.

   _____ III. It is better for visitors to be too formal than to be too informal.

4. Notice the clear transition (or bridge of thought) between the first section of the essay and the second: "Yet in spite of all the informality . . ." Notice, too, the clear statement of the second main point. How do the authors state it?

5. a. Is the central idea of the third section of the essay stated at the beginning of the discussion of that main point or at the end?

   b. How is the third point stated?

VI. Composition

OF INTERMEDIATE DIFFICULTY

Write a paragraph beginning with one of the following topic sentences, and develop the idea in it. You may take examples from the essay or give your own. The essay may also give you suggestions on wording, but do not merely copy the essay.

1. In spite of a certain amount of surface informality, the United States is not without customs that show deference or politeness of employee toward employer, of a younger person toward an older, of a man toward a woman, and of a student toward a teacher.
2. The American idea of good sportsmanship sometimes results in an apparent modesty that is difficult for a person from another country to understand.

ADVANCED

Write a paragraph on a social custom in your own country.

AMERICA: A LOOK AT THE COUNTRY, I

Word Study

1. difference /dífərəns/
2. similarity /sɪməlǽrəti/
3. mountain /maʊntn/
4. plain, plateau, prairie /plen, plætó, préri/
5. tropical /trɑ́pɪkəl/
6. arctic /ɑ́rktɪk/
7. fertile /fɚtəl/
8. desert /dézərt/
9. densely /dénsli/
10. sparsely /spɑ́rsli/
11. moist, moisture /mɔɪst, mɔɪstʃər/
12. arid /ǽrɪd/
13. landscape /lǽndskep/
14. vegetation /vɛdʒətéʃən/
15. boundary /baʊndri/
16. missionary, mission /míʃəneri, mɪʃən/
17. architecture /ɑ́rkətɛktʃər/
18. irrigated /írəgetəd/
19. evaporation /ɪvæpəréʃən/
20. prosperous /prɑ́spərəs/
21. glacial /gléʃəl/
22. paradise /pérədaɪs/
23. grazing /grezɪŋ/

Words that may be learned in contrasting pairs:

1. *difference*	If one object is larger than another but both are
2. *similarity*	red, there is a *difference* in size but a *similarity* in color.
3. *mountain*	A *mountain* is high; a *plain* or *plateau* or *prairie*
4. *plain, plateau, prairie*	is lower.
5. *tropical*	*Tropical* weather is very hot, but *arctic* weather is
6. *arctic*	very cold.
7. *fertile*	Crops grow well in *fertile* country, but few plants
8. *desert*	will grow in the *desert*.
9. *densely*	New York City is *densely* populated, but a desert
10. *sparsely*	is *sparsely* populated.
11. *moist*	Where much rain falls the land is *moist*; where
12. *arid*	there is little rain the land is *arid*. (The related noun *moisture* is also used in this essay.)

Words related to words you already know (related words are given in parentheses):

13. *landscape*   The *landscape* is the general view of all the land. (land)
14. *vegetation*   The *vegetation* is the plant life present in a place. (vegetable)
15. *boundary*   The *boundary* is the edge of an area, the line that bounds it. (bound)

Words that may need definition:
16. *missionary, mission*   A *missionary* is a person sent by the church to another country to preach or teach. The *mission* is the group of buildings where he lives and teaches or preaches.
17. *architecture*   style of building; type of construction of a building
18. *irrigated*   a descriptive word for land watered not by rain but by men bringing water to it from lakes and rivers
19. *evaporation*   act of giving off moisture into the air, or act of turning to moisture because of the heat (There is *evaporation* of water when the sun shines on it.)
20. *prosperous*   having continued good fortune, successful (A *prosperous* businessman has a successful business which is bringing him a good deal of money.)
21. *glacial*   formed from a glacier, or mass of ice (A *glacial* lake is formed by the melting of a glacier.
22. *paradise*   a place of great beauty where everything is perfect (Heaven is called *paradise*.)
21. *grazing*   eating the grass in the field (Cattle graze.)

Reading Suggestions
To help you follow the idea and general development of what you read, whether in your own language or in a foreign language, determine the author's plan. To aid you in doing this, look for (1) the central idea of the material as a whole (2) the type of arrangement that the material follows, and (3) the topic sentences, or guideposts, that the author uses to help you see the main divisions of the central theme. This essay, which, along with Essay 4, will describe a trip across the United States from the west coast to the east coast, is organized spatially. Each paragraph, except for the first two, which are introductory, will describe an area further east than the area described in the previous paragraph. Look for transitional words that show you this organizational pattern.

AMERICA: A LOOK AT THE COUNTRY, I

1. The United States is a country of great *differences* (1). At the same

time it has surprising *similarities* (2) when one considers its size. The differences are partly a result of the geography. One cannot generalize about the weather, the *landscape* (13), or even the way of living because the nation occupies nearly half of a continent. From coast to coast the continental United States exclusive of Hawaii and Alaska covers 2807 miles at its greatest width and extends 1598 miles from the northern *boundary* (15) to the southern tip of Texas. In it can be found high *mountains* (3) and the flattest of *prairies* (4), *tropical* (5) heat and *arctic* (6) cold, *fertile* (7) valleys and *desert* (8) areas. There is a variety of natural resources. All sorts of products are raised, and there are industries of every kind. Some of the most *densely* (9) and most *sparsely* (10) populated areas of the world are found in the United States.

2. To go from San Francisco to New York City by car, you must travel more than 3000 miles. You cross many regions of the country, and each region has characteristics of its own. To see the country in detail, you must turn off the main road to explore the cities, towns, and places of scenic beauty. But by following a superhighway such as U.S. Highway 40 or Interstate 80, you can get a bird's-eye or general view of the country.

3. In California, where you begin your trip, the climate is usually mild all year. *California* is a Spanish word meaning "heat of the ovens." The influence of Spanish *missionaries* (16) who settled the area can be found along the route still known as *El Camino Real* ("the main highroad"). The names of cities in the San Francisco area such as Santa Barbara, San Mateo, San Jose, and San Francisco itself are Spanish. Remains of old Spanish *missions* (16) may be seen, and there is a Spanish influence in the *architecture* (17). Slightly south of Highway 40 is the famous fruit-raising area. California oranges, grapefruit, and lemons as well as many other fruit and vegetables are shipped all over the United States and to other parts of the world.

4. Soon, however, you leave these *moist* (11), fertile *plains* (4) and go up into the Sierra Nevada, with their snow-capped peaks and clear mountain lakes. From these, the train comes out onto a high, *arid* (12) *plateau* (4). This western plateau covers much of the area of Nevada, Arizona, and Utah, and parts of Idaho and Colorado. The breezes of the Pacific lose their *moisture* (11) as they hit the mountains, so there is little rainfall here and the *vegetation* (14) is sparse. The scenery is often very strange. In some places occasional heavy rains have made deep cuts in the sand, exposing rocky walls of red, brown, or yellow. In other areas the winds have blown the sand into strange formations that have become baked and hardened by the sun. The days are hot and the nights cool. There is agriculture in *irrigated* (18) valleys, but much of the area is so barren that it is difficult even to raise sheep on it. The region has gold, silver, copper, lead, and zinc

mines, however. Few people live in this region, but there are occasional bands of Navaho Indians. If you could take a side trip to the south, you would see the Pueblo Indians in Arizona and New Mexico living in houses made of clay baked by the sun. On this trip you might also pass the huge Hoover Dam irrigation project on the boundary between Nevada and Arizona and make a trip to the famous Grand Canyon of the Colorado River.

5. As your car proceeds further east, you cross the Salt Lake Desert, formed by the *evaporation* (19) of the Great Salt Lake. For miles and miles you will see nothing but sand and salt. Finally, you skirt the shore of the Great Salt Lake itself and come to modern and *prosperous* (20) Salt Lake City. From the state of Utah you enter Colorado and cross the Rocky Mountains through a pass 12,000 feet high. Here the scenery may remind you of Switzerland, with *glacial* (21) lakes and peaks rising to over 14,000 feet. The Rocky Mountain area of Colorado, Wyoming, and parts of Idaho and Montana is a *paradise* (22) for tourists and vacationers. There are all sorts of places for them to stay, from beautiful hotels to camp grounds where one may set up his own tent. On side roads you may find ghost mining towns, deserted since the end of the gold rush days in the 1870s. You emerge from the mountains at Denver, Colorado, called "the Queen City of the Plains." East of Denver for 200 miles you cross high, treeless plains used for cattle *grazing* (23) and large-scale wheat farming.

6. From Colorado you may continue on U.S. Highway 30 through Nebraska, Iowa, and Illinois on your way to Chicago. As you cross Nebraska, you gradually leave this empty country and enter a rich farming region of America. The land becomes fertile and well watered, and more trees appear. Nebraska has many golden wheat fields. In Iowa and Illinois, wheat and corn are important products, and much livestock is raised. The summers are warm and the winters cold. Since farms of 500 acres and larger are common, the population is still not dense, although cities become more frequent as you go further east. Their factories and packing houses employ many people. On a typical Iowa farm is a large white house made of wood. It is surrounded by a neat lawn. Behind it is a huge red or white barn which is usually larger than the house. The farmhouse usually has hot running water, electricity, central heating, and a television set. The farmer's wife, when she goes to town, may wear the same style of clothes as her sister in New York or Chicago. The farmer's children may go to the state university. (*978 words*)

EXERCISES

I. Comprehension of Details

Indicate whether each of the following statements is true or false by writing the letter T or F in the space provided.

_____ 1. The name *California* is of Indian origin.

_____ 2. California is famous mainly for its large crop of apples.

_____ 3. The climate of California is too cold for orange raising.

_____ 4. The vegetation is sparse on the western plateau across the Sierra Nevada mountains from California.

_____ 5. Silver, copper, lead, and zinc mines may be found in Nevada, Arizona, and Utah.

_____ 6. The Hoover Dam between Nevada and Arizona was built for purposes of irrigation.

_____ 7. The Salt Lake desert will probably get larger.

_____ 8. The climate of parts of New Mexico and Arizona accounts for its sparse population.

_____ 9. Salt Lake City is not modern and prosperous because it is in the middle of a desert.

_____ 10. Farmers' children now may enjoy many of the educational advantages of city children.

II. Skimming Exercise

In what paragraph of this essay is a discussion of each of the following to be found?

1. the climate in California
2. the farmlands of America
3. the scenery in the Rocky Mountains
4. the high plateau country of the west
5. in general, the similarities and differences in the scenery in America

III. Vocabulary Exercises

WORD STUDY

Without referring to the word list at the beginning of this selection, write a word that contrasts in meaning with each of the following.

1. fertile   4. sparse   6. difference
2. tropical   5. arid   7. poor
3. plateau

Without referring to the word list, write a word related to each of the following.

1. vegetable   5. prosperous   8. evaporate
2. moist   6. glacier   9. bound
3. construct   7. irrigate   10. land
4. architect

Use in a sentence each of the words you have written in the preceding two exercises.

IDIOMATIC AND FIGURATIVE LANGUAGE
Circle the letter that precedes the item which most nearly defines the italicized expressions from the essay. The paragraph in which the expression is found is given in parentheses.
1. a *streamlined train* (2)
   a. a train with lines on it
   b. a train that goes near a river
   c. a train with no projecting parts to hinder its progress
2. a *bird's-eye view* (2)
   a. a view from a distance
   b. a view of a small part
   c. a rapid view
3. Fruits and vegetables are *shipped* all over the United States. (3)
   a. sent by ship
   b. sent by train, boat, or plane
   c. sent by water
4. a *side trip* (4)
   a. a trip beside something
   b. a trip away from the main route
   c. a trip in one direction
5. a *ghost town* (5)
   a. a deserted town
   b. a town of unknown origin
   c. a town with ghosts in it

IV. Comprehension of Grammatical Structure

EXERCISE A
Study paragraph 4 of the essay. Then close your book and complete the paragraph below by supplying the missing connectors, subordinators, and prepositions.

Soon, _____, you leave these moist, fertile plains and go up _____ the Sierra Nevada, _____ their snow-capped peaks and clear mountain lakes. _____ these, the train comes out _____ a high, arid plateau. This western plateau covers much _____ the area of Nevada, Arizona, and Utah, and parts _____ Idaho and Colorado. The breezes of the Pacific lose their moisture _____ they hit the mountains, so there is little rainfall here and the vegetation is sparse. The scenery is often very strange. _____ some places occasional heavy rains have made deep cuts _____ the sand, exposing rocky walls _____ red, brown, _____ yellow. _____ other areas the winds have blown the sand _____ strange formations that have become baked and hardened _____ the sun. The days are hot and the nights cool. There is agriculture _____ irrigated valleys, but much _____ the area is so barren _____ it is difficult even to raise sheep _____ it. The region has gold, silver, copper, lead, and zinc mines, _____. Few people live _____ this region, but there are occasional bands of Navaho Indians. _____ you could take a side trip _____ the south, you would see the Pueblo Indians in Arizona and New Mexico living _____ houses made of clay baked by the sun.

EXERCISE B

Could other words sometimes be substituted for the ones you have supplied in exercise A? Do the possible words usually belong to the same or to a different class of words? Give illustrations. For example, in the first space you could use *however, nevertheless, therefore, then.* All of these words are sentence connectors. (See Volume I, Appendix V.)

V. Comprehension of Main Ideas and Organizational Pattern

1. Place a check mark before whichever of the following is the best statement of the central idea of this essay.
   a. As you travel across the United States on a superhighway, you get a "general view" of the country.
   b. The United States is a country of great differences and surprising similarities.
   c. As you travel across the United States on a super–highway, you get a "general view" of the country that shows its great differences and surprising similarities.
   d. To go from San Francisco to New York City by car requires several days.
2. Place a check mark before whichever of the following statements best expresses the organizational pattern of this essay.
   a. The United States is a country of great differences. At the same time it has amazing similarities.
   b. Some of the most densely and some of the most sparsely populated areas of the world are found in the United States.
   c. To go from San Francisco to New York City by car, you must go more than 3000 miles.
   d. By driving from San Francisco to New York City, you can get a "general view" of the country.

3. We have noted that this essay is organized spatially. This organization begins in paragraph 3, after the introduction.
   a. The opening words of the first sentence in paragraph 3 shows this organization: "*In California, where you begin your trip,* the climate is usually mild all year." What area of the country will be discussed in paragraph 3?
   b. The opening words of paragraph 4 — "*Soon, however, you leave* these moist, fertile plains and go up into the Sierra Nevada" — continue to point out the spatial organization. What area of the country will be discussed in paragraph 4?
   c. What transitional words introduce paragraph 5 and show the spatial organization? What areas of the country will be discussed in this paragraph?
   d. What transitional words showing spatial organization do you find at the beginning of paragraph 6? What area of the country will be discussed in this paragraph?

VI. Composition

OF INTERMEDIATE DIFFICULTY

Write a composition answering one of the following questions.
1. What are some states one might travel through and what are some of the things one might see on a trip by bus or car from Chicago to San Francisco?
2. How does the scenery of Nevada, Arizona, and Colorado differ from that of Illinois, Iowa, or Nebraska?

ADVANCED

Describe the scenery in an area in your native country. Use spatial organization. What would you see as you cross the area from east to west, or from north to south?

AMERICA: A LOOK AT THE COUNTRY, II

Word Study

1. boulevard /búləvɑrd/
2. ripple /rípəl/
3. toll /tol/
4. population /pɑpyəléʃən/
5. mansion /mǽnʃən/
6. sharecroppers /ʃɛŕkrɑpərz/
7. provincial /prəvínʃəl/
8. residential /rɛzədénʃəl/
9. mobility /mobíləti/

The words in the above list may need definition.
1. *boulevard* a very wide street, often with large, beautiful buildings on it, and lined with trees and grass
2. *ripple* a small wave or roughness in the surface of the water.
3. *toll* a fee paid to travel on a road
4. *population* the whole number of people in the given area
5. *mansion* a large, expensive house
6. *sharecropper* a small farmer in southern United States who receives part of the crop in return for farming for another person
7. *provincial* having the ways of people who have never been very far from home or from their own region or province
8. *residential* adjectival form of *residence*, a place where one lives
9. *mobility* ease of movement (There is great *mobility* of the population in America because of the automobile.)

Reading Suggestions

This essay is a continuation of Essay 3, and will follow the same spatial order in the first four paragraphs. Paragraphs 5, 6, and 7 discuss other regions of the country not covered on the trip from west to east. The final paragraph is a conclusion. Note its relationship to the first paragraph of the previous essay.

AMERICA: A LOOK AT THE COUNTRY, II

1. You have now traveled many days and spent many nights perhaps in motels—motor hotels that dot the country. These motels

are usually air-conditioned, even when located far from a major city, and often provide a swimming pool for the children, or tired adults, to frolic in at the end of a long day's driving. Now you find your way through a mass of busy superhighways into the bustling city of Chicago. As in any big city, the streets are usually crowded with traffic at whatever hour you arrive. If your route takes you near the shore of Lake Michigan, you will travel a broad *boulevard* (1) with eight lanes of fast-moving traffic along the waterfront. Tall office buildings and hotels are on your left, and on your right *ripple* (2) the blue waters of the lake. Further back from the lake, you see narrow, crowded streets lined with rows and rows of red brick houses. Vegetable sellers push little carts through the streets and call out the names of things for sale in any one of a number of languages.

2. Chicago, with an interracial *population* (4), is a center of industry and culture for the middle part of the country. Not only are there steel mills and factories, but also museums and universities. The Chicago Art Institute is world famous.

3. Leaving Chicago, you cross Indiana, Ohio, Pennsylvania, and New Jersey to go to New York City. These are agricultural states also, but the number of large cities and the amount of industry increases as you continue east. In Pennsylvania you cross the Appalachian Mountains, which are considerably lower than the Rockies. They are a center of the coal-mining industry. Should you desert one of the major cross-country freeways or *toll* (3) roads, you will see beautiful country homes in the rolling, wooded hills, or pass through little mining towns with rows of wooden houses dirty with smoke. Pennsylvania and New Jersey constitute the richest industrial region of the country.

4. New York City, your destination, is perhaps the least typically "American" of any American city, because more than half of its population is foreign-born or of foreign parentage. There are almost half a million first- and second-generation Italians living here, and as many Russians. One-fourth of the population is Jewish. There are large Puerto Rican areas. Yet, Wall Street with its stock market and banking establishments and Broadway with its theaters characterize New York as the financial and cultural heart of the United States.

5. This trip will not show you all of America, of course. The South, made up of the states of Virginia, Tennessee, North and South Carolina, Georgia, Alabama, Mississippi, Louisiana, and Florida, has been an agricultural region, raising most of the nation's cotton and tobacco. Recently many factories have been built there.

6. This is a land of contrasts. Here you may still find the large plantation *mansion* (5), a relic of a past century. Characteristic is a porch supported by white pillars. The house is often surrounded by a garden beautiful in the spring with masses of flowering shrubs. In

the South also are unpainted shacks of white or black *sharecroppers* (6) and farmers, with little tobacco or cotton fields beside them.

7. Other interesting trips might be taken to the forest areas of northern Minnesota, Wisconsin, and Michigan, or to the states of Washington and Oregon on the Pacific Coast. In northern Minnesota you can drive for miles and miles down narrow roads which seem to tunnel through the tall pine trees. Many of these trees are original forest and rise 40 or 50 feet high. Through the trees you may see the blue waters of one of the ten thousand lakes that Minnesota boasts of. Sometimes you may pass an Indian camp, but often you can go all day without seeing another person except perhaps vacationers like yourself. The states of Washington and Oregon have mountains and sea in addition to the forests to attract tourists.

8. Each region of the United States has characteristics of its own. There are large and modern cities, but a great proportion of the country consists of open land dotted with farmhouses and small *provincial* (7) towns. However, there are striking uniformities in the American scene that surprise foreign observers. There is an appearance of the country as a whole that might be said to be typically American. The usual town of average size, in any part of the United States, has its "main street" with the same types of stores selling the same products. Branches of big stores such as Montgomery Ward or Sears, Roebuck may be found in nearly every town. Every town has the same type of drugstore and supermarket. There is some variety of architecture, due to the differences in climate, locality, and national backgrounds of the people. Yet many American *residential* (8) areas, especially new ones, tend to have a similar look. Houses of brick, stone, or wood are set apart from each other by a grass plot or "yard." Generally there is no fence or hedge to separate them. In many ways Cheyenne, Wyoming, will resemble Rochester, New York, or Montgomery, Alabama. The similarities result from the extreme *mobility* (9) of the population and the free interchange of goods. There are differences in the manners and customs of the people, but there are common ways of thinking also. We will talk about some of these in the following essays. (*990 words*)

EXERCISES

I. Comprehension of Details

Without referring to the essay, complete the following statements about it.

1. One of the largest industries in Chicago mentioned in this essay is _____.

2. The Appalachian Mountains in Pennsylvania are a center for the
_____ industry.
3. There is a large foreign-born population in the state of _____.
4. Two important agricultural crops of the South are _____ and
_____.
5. The tourist attractions of the states of Washington and Oregon
are _____ and _____.
6. The state of _____ is famous for its ten thousand lakes.
7. Some of the uniformities in American towns result from _____
and _____.

II. Skimming Exercise

As quickly as possible, find the number of the paragraph or paragraphs that discuss each of the following.
1. forests in the northern part of the United States
2. contrasts in the South
3. the industrial region of the United States
4. the city of Chicago
5. reasons for similarities in the American scene

III. Vocabulary Exercise

WORD STUDY

To see whether you understand the meanings of the italicized words,
indicate whether each of the following statements is true or false by
writing T or F in the space provided.
____1. A very rich person usually lives in a *mansion*.
____2. The business district of a large American city is the main
residential area.
____3. All of the small towns in the United States could be described
as *spectacular*.
____4. Sometimes mountain people do not have a chance to travel
and are therefore *provincial*.
____5. In the country you usually find many *boulevards*.
____6. Trains, planes, and cars contribute to the *mobility* of the
American people.
____7. The *population* of Chicago is greater than that of New York
City.

IDIOMATIC AND FIGURATIVE LANGUAGE

Circle the letter preceding the sentence in which the italicized word
is used in the same sense as it was used in this essay. Numbers in
parentheses refer to paragraphs in the essay where the word or expression is found.
1. You see beautiful country homes in the *rolling*, wooded hills. (3)

  a. The ball was *rolling* down the street.
  b. The *rolling* surface of the ocean was beautiful in the sunlight.
  c. A *rolling* stone gathers no moss.
2. After leaving Chicago, you *cross* Indiana. (3)
  a. You must *cross* the street to get there.
  b. The teacher is very *cross*.
  c. Be sure to *cross* out the wrong answer.
3. The Old South is *made up* of Virginia, Tennessee, North and South Carolina, Georgia, Alabama, Mississippi, Louisiana, and Florida. (5)
  a. They kissed and *made up*.
  b. The student who had been absent *made up* the examination.
  c. Students from ten countries *made up* the class.
4. Often you can *go* all day without seeing another person. (7)
  a. Some people cannot *go* for a long time without a cigarette.
  b. A camel can *go* without water for a long time.
  c. Don't *go* on your vacation without your raincoat.

IV. Comprehension of Grammatical Structure

Without looking at the essay, in each of the blanks in the following paragraph supply the suitable auxiliary verb(s) or the correct form of the verb in parentheses.

Other interesting trips _____ taken to the forest areas of northern Minnesota, Wisconsin, and Michigan, or to the states of Washington and Oregon on the Pacific coast. In northern Minnesota you _____ drive for miles and miles down narrow roads which seem _____ (tunnel) through the tall pine trees. Many of these trees are original forest and _____ (rise) 40 or 50 feet high. Through the trees you _____ see the blue waters of one of the ten thousand lakes that Minnesota _____ (boast) of. Sometimes you _____ pass an Indian camp, but often you _____ go all day without _____ (see) another person except perhaps vacationers like yourself. The states of Washington and Oregon _____ (have) mountains and sea in addition to the forests _____ (attract) tourists.

V. Comprehension of Main Ideas and Organizational Pattern

MAIN IDEAS
1. Paragraphs 1 and 2 discuss Chicago. Do both paragraphs deal with exactly the same aspect of the topic? If not, what is the difference between the ideas in each of these two paragraphs?
2. According to paragraph 3, what two characteristics do the states of Indiana, Ohio, Pennsylvania, and New Jersey have in common? How do they differ?

3. What are three characteristics that Pennsylvania, New Jersey, and New York have in common, according to paragraph 4?
4. What area of the country does paragraph 5 deal with?
5. What is the topic of paragraph 6? How is it similar to that of paragraph 5? How is it different?
6. What two areas of the country are discussed in paragraph 7? What is the relationship between these areas?
7. What idea is discussed in paragraph 8 that is also discussed in the first paragraph of Essay 3?
8. Give two examples of this idea that are given in paragraph 8.

ORGANIZATIONAL PATTERN

This essay departs from west–east spatial organization in paragraphs 5, 6, 7. Note how this division is introduced in paragraph 5: "This trip will not show you all of America, of course. You must also . . ."

1. What transitional word at the beginning of paragraph 6 joins it to paragraph 5?
2. What transitional words introduce paragraph 7?
3. Paragraph 8 is a summary of Essays 3 and 4. Select again the topic sentence for the two essays as expressed in the opening paragraph of Essay 3. What words and ideas in paragraph 8 refer to this idea?

Essay 5

AMERICA: A LOOK AT THE PEOPLE

Word Study

1. previously /prívɪəsli/
2. predominant /pridámənənt/
3. generation /dʒɛnəréʃən/
4. application /æplɪkéʃən/
5. registration /rɛdʒəstréʃən/
6. vacation /vekéʃən/
7. institution /ɪnstətúʃən/
8. modification /mɑdəfɪkéʃən/
9. exaggeration /ɪgzædʒəréʃən/
10. reputation /rɛpyətéʃən/
11. illustrate /íləstret/
12. assimilate /əsíməlet/
13. isolate /aísəlet/
14. traditional /trədíʃənəl/
15. cultural /kəltʃərəl/
16. provincialism /prəvínʃəlɪzm/
17. nationality /næʃənǽləti/
18. identity /aɪdéntəti/
19. diversity /daɪvə́rsɪti/
20. patriotic /petrɪɑ́tɪk/
21. ancestor /ǽnsɛstər/
22. immigration /ɪməgréʃən/
23. tend /tɛnd/

The most commonly used words in the English language are usually Germanic in origin. They come from an older form of English called Anglo-Saxon, spoken in England from the time of the Germanic migration in the fifth century until after the conquest by the Norman French in 1066. After 1066 many French words based on Latin came into the English language, and words that are literary rather than spoken came from Latin. If you know Latin, French, or Spanish, the meaning of many of the words in the preceding list will be clear to you. The words may be grouped by common prefixes, suffixes, or roots. Related words are given in parentheses.

pre- Latin prefix meaning "before" or "first"
 1. *previously* at an earlier time (previous)
 2. *predominant* having power above others (predominance, predominate)

-tion, -ation ending or suffix indicating a noun and meaning "act of" or "condition of"
 3. *generation* the whole group of individuals born about the same time (generate)

41

4. *application*   act of putting to a special use or purpose (apply)
5. *registration*   act of making an official record (register)
6. *vacation*   a holiday period, time off from work (vacate — act of making empty)
7. *institution*   an organization or establishment for the purpose of promoting a certain object (institute — act of establishing)
8. *modification*   act of changing form or quality to some degree (modify)
9. *exaggeration*   act of overstating, or making large beyond the limits of truth (exaggerate)
10. *reputation*   the opinion held about a person or thing by the community (repute)

-ate   suffix indicating a verb. The related noun usually ends in *-ation*.
11. *illustrate*   to draw, or provide a picture or example of (illustration)
12. *assimilate*   to take in, absorb, or incorporate as one's own (assimilation)
13. *isolate*   to set apart, or detach, or separate from others (isolation)

-al   suffix indicating an adjective
14. *traditional*   according to established custom (tradition)
15. *cultural*   pertaining to cultivation, education, development (culture)

-ism   suffix indicating a noun and meaning "stage of"
16. *provincialism*   state of being from the provinces, or acting as though one came from the provinces (provincial) (Examples of other words that follow this form are: traditional-traditionalism, institutional-institutionalism.)

-ity   suffix indicating a noun and meaning "state of" or "condition of"
17. *nationality*   state of belonging to a nation (nation, national, nationalism)
18. *identity*   the condition or fact of being oneself or itself and not another (identify, identification)
19. *diversity*   state of showing many different forms (diverse, diversify, diversification)

-ic   suffix indicating an adjective
20. *patriotic*   loving and serving one's country (patriot) (Examples of other words that follow this form are: character — characteristic, diplomat — diplomatic.)

ancestr-   combined form of two Latin word roots meaning "coming before"
21. *ancestor*   a person who has lived before you and from whom you are descended (ancestry [group of ancestors], ancestral)

migr- Latin root meaning "to move"
22. *immigration* act of moving into a locality by a group of people
(immigrant [person who moves in], migration [act of moving])

tend- Latin root meaning "to extend" or "to have a direction toward
any place or object or end"
23. *tend* to incline to go in a certain direction, or toward a certain
object (tendency)

Reading Suggestions
Read as rapidly as you can to note details about the population of the
United States. Check difficult constructions for further discussion.

AMERICA: A LOOK AT THE PEOPLE

1. In a gathering of friends in the United States, in a meeting of a
business or educational organization, or at a public meeting, the
family names of the people present might reveal something about the
diversity of national backgrounds that they represent. The mixture
of national backgrounds would differ somewhat in different parts of
the country. Many Scandinavians live in Minnesota, and there are
many Irish in Boston, Massachusetts. New York City is the *traditional*
(14) "melting pot." The South is heavily British and these people
have been in America for many generations. Many Spanish and
Mexicans are found in the Southwest. Yet a mixture of *nationalities*
(17) is characteristic of the fabric of American society. Mills, O'Fallon,
Tognozzini, Zimmerman, Hoshida, Havlika, Zimanski, Gruber, or
Ten Brink — all are American names, and the country is a blend of all
the *cultural* (15) strains these names represent.
2. The differences in nationality within the American pattern may
be *illustrated* (11) by the fact that it is not uncommon for one American
to say to another, "What nationality are you?" meaning, "What
country did your ancestors come from?" *Application* (4) blanks for
jobs and *registration* (5) forms for schools often contain a space labeled
"Nationality _____." An American may fill the blank with "German,"
"Polish," "Italian," or "English," although he was born in the United
States and neither he nor perhaps even his parents or grandparents
may have ever gone outside the country, unless for a summer *vacation* (6) trip to the Canadian side of Niagara Falls. That these people
write down the national origin of their ancestors rather than the
name of the land in which they were born does not mean that they
are not *patriotic* (20) Americans. It merely means that they are still
conscious of their differences in ancestry. This feeling of *identity* (18)
with the cultural background of one's ancestors along with a pride

in being an American has long been a characteristic of the American people. American culture is the product of many different cultures blended together to form something new.

3. This new culture is not just a *modification* (8) of the culture of one European country or a mixture of several. The English came first and for many years were *predominant* (2). British *institutions* (7) have influenced the formation of American ones. But this original British character has been modified first by life in a new land and then by the coming of people from other countries. Though in 1790, when the first census was taken, 69 percent of the population was of British origin, even then the American people were no longer British. Something had happened to them in the new land.

4. Since 1790 the British predominance in national background has been greatly modified. The most common American family names such as Jones, Brown, Smith, and Johnson are English. However, for a majority of Americans England is no longer "our old home" as it was for the writer Nathaniel Hawthorne a century ago. The great *immigration* (22) from other countries began in the early nineteenth century. Before 1860 the people came largely from northern and western Europe or Canada. The potato famine in Ireland brought one-fifth of the population of Ireland (1,500,000 people) to the United States between 1840 and 1855. In the 1850s the Germans were the chief immigrants. In the latter part of the nineteenth century new streams from other areas came in. In 1870, 123,000 Chinese entered the United States, largely to work as laborers on the west coast. Between 1880 and 1910 most of the migration came from southern and eastern Europe. During this period the United States received 3,000,000 Italians, 2,000,000 Russians, and 1,500,000 Jews, 71 percent of whom came from Russia. The mingling of all these people in a new country has produced a new culture, some aspects of which we shall discuss in the paragraphs that follow.

5. The time at which these various groups came has influenced the extent to which they have mixed into American society. Many of the more recently immigrating groups have found employment as factory workers in large cities, and people from a given country *tend* (23) to find housing in the same area. San Francisco has its Chinatown complete with its own telephone exchange and daily newspaper. The Polish and Italian sections of Chicago are second only to Warsaw and Milan in the number of inhabitants from those countries. Los Angeles has a Mexican population second only to Mexico City. New York has a larger Jewish population than any other city in the world. More than half of all New Yorkers are either foreign-born or of foreign-born parents. In that city there are sections called "Little Italy," "Little Poland," and "Little Russia." It is therefore no surprise that in New York City newspapers are pub-

lished in two hundred languages besides English. Wherever such national groups are gathered, it is only natural that they remain a group apart. They speak their native language among themselves and preserve their old customs. Thus older groups in the United States tend to regard these recent immigrants as foreigners, a tendency disappearing as the groups become *assimilated* (12). Since recent immigrants came largely from southern Europe or countries such as Greece, Italy, or the Slavic countries, it is the Italians and Greeks or Hungarians and Slavic people who are commonly so termed. The older groups are often made up of people originally as poor as or poorer than the newcomers; but because they have been in America longer, they have been able to develop the resources of the area and rise to positions of dominance in the community.

6. In spite of this tendency, however, America is not deeply divided socially according to national background or the length of time one's ancestors have lived in this country. This is particularly true after the first generation. Immigrants gradually become assimilated. Differences of national background have become more a matter of pride than of social distinction and do not hold groups apart from the community.

7. Regional rather than national differences often characterize the people of certain areas and add another element of *diversity* (19) to the population of America. The works of American poets, authors, musicians, and artists often reflect their ancestral background or portray typical features of the region where they live. *Exaggeration* (9) of regional differences forms the basis of much American humor. The New Englanders who have lived for generations on rocky soil have had to labor hard to gain a living from their farms. They have a *reputation* (10), not wholly correct, for being silent and stern and careful with their money. Texas is so big that Texans think of everything connected with the state as being equally large: all ranches are as big as counties and every man is at least 8 feet tall and lights his cigar with a thousand-dollar bill. It is true that Texas is favored in natural resources, but neither the state nor the people are quite as big as the natives would have you think.

8. In certain *isolated* (13) mountain regions, particularly in the East, there are people whose poor farms and lack of contact with the outside world have bred poverty and *provincialism* (16). The people are called "mountaineers," and the popular conception is that they never wear shoes, are always fighting with the neighbors, and will shoot a stranger on sight. There are elements of truth and of exaggeration in this picture also.

9. With all of these groups making up the American people, it may seem surprising that American society is as uniform as it is. American culture has typical features, and perhaps one of the most

characteristic is the blending of all the diverse strains to produce distinctive American customs and ideals. (*1277 words*)

EXERCISES

I. Comprehension of Details

Indicate whether each of the following statements is true or false by writing the letter T or F in the space provided.

_____ 1. The proportion of people of English ancestry in America has decreased since 1790.

_____ 2. English names predominate in the United States.

_____ 3. There are some regional differences in American culture, as, for example, in the Southwest, Texas, and eastern mountain areas.

_____ 4. American society has little uniformity because of the great diversity of regional and cultural differences.

_____ 5. American citizens may be regarded as foreigners if they remain with their own national group and speak their own native language.

_____ 6. Americans tend to consider themselves first Norwegians, Germans, or Armenians, depending upon their national background, rather than Americans.

_____ 7. Many recent immigrants find employment as factory workers in the East.

_____ 8. There is no truth to the stories one hears about mountaineers or Texans.

_____ 9. The family name of a person in the United States may not accurately show his national background.

_____10. An American artist may portray typical characteristics of the area where he lives that have little to do with the national background of the people.

II. Skimming Exercise

As quickly as possible, find the number of the paragraph(s) in which each of the following is mentioned or discussed.

1. the influence of English migration on American culture
2. an American's attitude toward his nationality
3. influences of regional rather than national differences in the American culture pattern
4. assimilation of culture groups in American society

III. Vocabulary Exercise

1. Name four English words with prefix *pre-* (meaning "before").
2. Give the noun meaning "act of" which can be formed from each

of the following verbs: *assimilate, dominate, isolate, characterize*
3. Name two adjectives (not in the Word Study) with an *-al* ending. Name two adjectives (not in the Word Study) with an *-ic* ending. (These may be formed from some of the words in the Word Studies of the preceding essays.)
4. Name all the words you can think of that are formed on the same root as each of the following: *domin*ant, *migra*tory, *identifi*cation, *simil*ar.
5. In the following choose the best meaning in parentheses for each of the italicized words.
    a. They attended the state university together *previously* (at the same time, earlier, sooner, happily).
    b. Their *ancestors* (relatives, friends, forefathers, grandfathers) have lived in the United States for five generations.
    c. These groups have been *assimilated* into (made part of, identified with, educated, forced into) American culture so that they have become a part of it.
    d. These people are *patriotic* (dominant, foreign, loyal, naturalized) Americans.
    e. *Exaggerations* (pictures, characterizations, overstatements, numbers) of regional differences are a cause for humor in the United States.
    f. There is a great *diversity* (number, distribution, difference, size) of national groups in America.
    g. The people in certain mountain areas of America have been *isolated* (separated, warned against, different, identified with).

IV. Comprehension of Grammatical Structure
In each of the blanks in the following sentences taken from the essay, supply *which, when, who, whom, what,* or *that.* The number at the end of each sentence refers to the paragraph from which the sentence is taken. When you have finished, check your sentences with those in the essay.
1. The differences in nationality within the American pattern may be illustrated by the fact _____ it is not uncommon for one American to say to another, "_____ nationality are you?" (2)
2. During this period the United States received 1,500,000 Jews, 71 percent of _____ came from Russia. (4)
3. The mingling of all these people in a new country has produced a new culture, some aspects of _____ we shall discuss in the paragraphs that follow. (4)
4. The time at _____ these various groups came has influenced the extent to _____ they have mixed into American society. (5)
5. The people are called "mountaineers," and the popular concep-

tion is _____ they never wear shoes and are always fighting with
their neighbors. (8)

V. Comprehension of Main Ideas and Organizational Pattern
Quote the sentence in the indicated paragraph which gives the best
answer to each of the following questions.
1. What is the best statement of the central idea of the selection?
   (paragraph 1)
2. What other statement of the same idea can you find? Where?
3. What is the relationship between American and British culture?
   (paragraph 3)
4. How has this culture been modified by people from other countries? (paragraph 4)
5. What is the relationship between national background and social
   status (a) when new groups first come in? (paragraph 5) and (b) as
   new groups become assimilated? (paragraph 6)
6. To what extent are there regional differences in the United States,
   and how important are they? (paragraph 7)

VI. Composition

OF INTERMEDIATE DIFFICULTY
Write a paragraph developing one of the following topic sentences.
1. The United States is made up of people from many different
   national groups.
2. Regional as well as national differences are an important element
   in the cultural pattern of the United States.

ADVANCED
Write a short essay (about 500 words) on one of the following topics.
1. Different Types of People in My Country
2. Regional Differences in the Cultural Pattern of My Country

Essay 6

A STORY OF THE WEST

Word Study

1. glamour /glǽmər/
2. frontier /frəntír/
3. unique /yuník/
4. episode /ɛ́pəsod/
5. adorn /ədɔ́rn/
6. scroll /skrol/
7. drabness /drǽbnəs/
8. notorious /notóriəs/
9. saloon /səlún/
10. lure /lʊr/
11. rumor /rúmər/
12. prospective /prəspɛ́ktɪv/
13. persistent /pərsístənt/
14. thrifty /θrífti/
15. honeymoon /hɔ́nɪmun/
16. extravagant /ɛkstrǽvəgənt/

Try to determine the meaning of these words by the way they are used in the following sentences.
1. The West is a land of *glamour*, according to the movies. It has excitement and romance.
2. The *frontier* is the edge of settlement. Beyond it is wilderness. Alaska is the last frontier of the United States.
3. Leadville, Colorado, is *unique*. There is no other city like it.
4. An exciting *episode* took place at the theater last night. I have never seen a happening like it.
5. The house was decorated and *adorned* with many ornaments.
6. The houses are decorated with *scrolls*, or curling designs.
7. The house was a dull gray. Its *drabness* contrasted with the bright yellow of the house next to it.
8. A hero is famous, but a criminal is *notorious*.
9. A *saloon* is a place where liquor is served. It is a rather old-fashioned name for such a place.
10. A desire for gold *lured* many people to California. It made them want to go there.
11. A *rumor* is a story that may or may not be true. It is usually an exciting story, and so people tell it to their friends.
12. The prospects, or possibilities, of finding gold in California were good in 1849. Many *prospective* gold miners went there, hoping to find gold.
13. Small boys are *persistent* questioners. They persist in asking questions. They ask them all the time.

14. A *thrifty* person saves his money. He does not spend it freely.
15. Many people take a trip to Niagara Falls after they are married. That is a favorite place for a *honeymoon*.
16. An *extravagant* person spends his money freely and sometimes foolishly. He is not thrifty.

Reading Suggestions

This selection tells a story. The events are presented in the order in which they occur in time. This type of organization is called *chrono-logical*. Material organized in this way often does not have topic sentences which are as clearly stated as they must be in material that is organized logically, that is, by ideas or topics. The time arrangement guides you from one fact to another. Look for the markers (*finally, later,* etc.) that show time progression.

A STORY OF THE WEST

It has been over 350 years since the first settlements in the United States were made by Europeans. People now look back upon the country's history and the old colorful figures who, in a sense, typified a given area. The story that follows concerns two famous characters who were part of the Rocky Mountain gold-rush days. Their story has been made the subject of a popular American opera: *The Ballad of Baby Doe* by John Latouche, with music by Douglas Stuart Moore.

1. The West is traditionally the land of *glamour* (1) and romance in America — the land of the pioneers and the cowboys, of the gold rush and the land rush, where fortunes could be easily made and lost and made again in cattle or land or mining. Now much of the country is enclosed by fences, the covered wagon is replaced by the automobile and modern cities take the place of *frontier* (2) settlements. The cabins of the pioneers and miners are gone. A few "old-time" cowboys remain, but many of the cowboys' sons are students at a university or state agricultural school. There are still places, however, where the spirit of the Old West remains. One of these is the mining town of Leadville, Colorado.

2. Leadville is *unique* (3) in being the highest city in the United States. It is located in the Rocky Mountains and is 10,000 feet above sea level. Its most unusual feature, however, is the living picture of the past which it preserves. Leadville is not really old in years. It has existed less than a century, but it recalls an *episode* (4) in the history of the West. When the town was in its heyday, as late as 1890, it had a population of some 40,000 living in wooden houses of similar architecture, *adorned* (5) with wooden *scrolls*. Now only about 5000 live there and occupy the old houses. Many of the buildings are in disrepair and in need of paint, and since the town is close to the

timberline, there is a certain bareness to its appearance apart from the *drabness* (7) of its houses. Nevertheless, there is a romantic glamour there. The big hotel, the Tabor opera house, and even some of the *notorious* (8) *saloons* (9) are still used, and one can imagine how life was lived in the days when every citizen hoped to become a millionaire.

3. Among the more colorful characters of Leadville's golden age were H. A. W. Tabor and his second wife, Elizabeth McCourt, better known as "Baby Doe." Their history is fast becoming one of the legends of the Old West. Horace Austin Warner Tabor was a schoolteacher in Vermont. With his first wife and two children he left Vermont by covered wagon in 1855 to homestead in Kansas. Perhaps he did not find farming to his liking, or perhaps he was *lured* (10) by *rumors* (11) of fortunes to be made in Colorado mines. At any rate, a few years later he moved west to the small Colorado mining camp known as California Gulch, which he later renamed Leadville when he became its leading citizen. "Great deposits of lead are sure to be found here," he said.

4. As it turned out, it was silver, not lead, that was to make Leadville's fortune and his. Tabor knew little about mining himself, so he opened a general store, which sold everything from boots to salt, flour, and tobacco. It was his custom to "grubstake" *prospective* (12) miners, in other words to supply them with food and supplies, or "grub," while they looked for ore, in return for which he would get a share in the mine if one was discovered. He did this for a number of years, but no one that he aided ever found anything of value.

5. Finally one day in the year 1878, so the story goes, two miners came in and asked for "grub." Tabor had decided to quit supplying it because he had lost too much money that way. These miners were *persistent* (13), however, and Tabor was too busy to argue with them. "Oh, help yourself. One more time won't make any difference," he said and went on selling shoes and hats to other customers. The two miners took seventeen dollars' worth of supplies, in return for which they gave Tabor a one-third interest in their findings. They picked a barren place on the mountain side and began to dig. After nine days they struck a rich vein of silver. Tabor bought the shares of the other two men, and so the mine belonged to him alone. This mine, known as the "Pittsburg Mine," made $1,300,000 for Tabor in return for his seventeen-dollar investment.

6. Later Tabor bought the Matchless Mine on another barren hillside just outside of the town for $117,000. This turned out to be even more fabulous than the Pittsburg, yielding $35,000 worth of silver per day at one time. Leadville grew. Tabor became its first mayor, and later became lieutenant governor of the state. At this time he met Baby Doe, a beautiful young girl with blonde curls and

big blue eyes. His wife had too many New England virtues. She was *thrifty* (14) and carefully saved the money she earned from doing laundry for the miners. She was an excellent housekeeper. She kept things neat and tidy and made Tabor wipe his feet before entering the house. He gave her $1,200,000 as a divorce settlement and secretly married Baby Doe. Later he became United States senator, and they were married publicly in a big ceremony in Washington. Mr. Chester A. Arthur, President of the United States, attended. Tabor was 53 years old at the time, and Baby Doe was 21. The *honeymoon* (15) cost $10,000 a day. As a wedding gift he gave her the famed Isabella Diamond, supposed to have been sold by Queen Isabella of Spain to pay for Columbus' voyage on which he discovered America. Tabor bought himself a $250 nightshirt. Leadville was too small for the Tabors. They moved to Denver, where Tabor built the city a million-dollar opera house, then the finest between St. Louis and San Francisco, but now torn down to make room for a modern office building.

7. All went well until 1893, the year of the silver panic. The United States no longer used silver as a standard for coinage. With the price of silver down, Tabor could not afford to operate the Matchless Mine. He had spent all of his money in *extravagant* (16) living and had to go to work as a day laborer in Denver. It is reported that one time when he and Baby Doe had nothing in the house to eat, his first wife, living comfortably on her $1,200,000, sent them a wagon load of food, enough to keep them all winter.

8. During the last year of his life his friends got him a job as a clerk in the Denver post office, which his money had built. When he died in 1899, his last words to Baby Doe were "Hang on to the Matchless. It will make you a fortune." Baby Doe did what Tabor told her, and she moved into a little shack at the entrance to the mine. The shack is still there. It has been repaired, but otherwise it is much as it was when she lived there. There is a cot, a table, and one or two chairs. A small coal stove sits in one corner. On the walls are a few pots and pans. There is a Catholic altar against one wall, with some candles and a cross on it. Letters of Baby Doe's, which are preserved in a case at one side of the room, indicate that in her last years she seldom left the shack for fear that someone would try to enter the mine. Friends brought her a small supply of food and coal. To keep track of time, she marked off the days on her calendar, which still hangs on the wall. In the middle of March, 1935, the markings stopped. The frozen body of the 73-year-old woman was found a few days later, still guarding the Matchless Mine. (*1346 words*)

EXERCISES

I. Comprehension of Details

Indicate which choice best completes each of the following statements.
1. Leadville is (a) a very old city, (b) a very new city, (c) less than one hundred years old, (d) about fifty years old.
2. Leadville is now (a) an exciting place to live, (b) old and drab in appearance, (c) glamorous because of its beauty, (d) a city of large modern homes.
3. The present population of Leadville is (a) about 40,000, (b) about the same as in 1890, (c) larger than in 1890, (d) very much smaller than in 1890.
4. When Tabor came to Leadville, he worked as a (a) farmer, (b) miner, (c) postal clerk, (d) storekeeper.
5. He made his first fortune by (a) prospecting for silver, (b) finding a lead mine, (c) supporting two prospectors who found a silver mine, (d) running a store.
6. Tabor divorced his first wife because (a) she kept house too well, (b) she took in the miners' laundry after he became rich, (c) she was extravagant, (d) she did not keep house well.
7. Among Baby Doe's wedding presents was (a) the Matchless Mine, (b) Queen Isabella's diamond, (c) a million-dollar opera house, (d) a $250 dress.
8. Tabor lost his fortune because (a) the Matchless Mine failed to produce more silver, (b) he spent his money extravagantly, (c) he "grubstaked" too many prospectors, (d) the United States no longer used silver as a standard for coinage.
9. During the last year of his life Tabor (a) had a job as a postal clerk, (b) lived on money sent by his first wife, (c) starved to death, (d) lived in a shack by the Matchless Mine.
10. Baby Doe (a) died soon after Tabor, (b) lived comfortably on money and food supplied during her last years by Tabor's first wife, (c) reopened the Matchless Mine, (d) became a recluse in her last years and seldom left her home.

II. Skimming Exercise

You will find that you can read this selection more rapidly than you can read some of the others because you are reading it for the story rather than for detailed factual information. After you have read it once and mastered the difficulties, time yourself on a second reading to see how quickly you can comprehend what you read.

III. Vocabulary Exercises

WORD STUDY
1. Note the following formations: *drab*—adjective, *drabness*—noun. On the same pattern, make nouns of the following adjectives from the Word Study list: (a) unique, (b) thrifty (note that final *y* changes to *i* before an ending), (c) notorious. Use the words you have formed in sentences.
2. In the space provided at the beginning of each of the following sentences write the part of speech (noun, verb, adjective, adverb) for the italicized word in the sentence.

    _____a. He was *lured* to the West by rumors of gold.

    _____b. The *lure* of the West has caused many people to cross the country.

    _____c. The *rumor* of fortunes to be made brought many people to the West.

    _____d. They *rumor* that gold can be found in California.

IDIOMATIC AND FIGURATIVE LANGUAGE
In each of the following circle the letter preceding the phrase or sentence that best expresses the meaning of the italicized word as used in this narrative. You may want to refer to the paragraph in which the item occurs to see how it is used in context.
1. When the town was in its *heyday* (2)
   a. old age
   b. period of greatest prosperity and success
   c. decline
2. Since the town is close to the *timberline* (2)
   a. the level on the mountain where the trees end
   b. the level on the mountain where the trees begin
   c. the railroad on which the timber is shipped
3. Had to go to work as a *day laborer* (7)
   a. a person who works only for a day
   b. a person who gets paid by the day
   c. a person who works only during the day
4. *Hang on* to the Matchless (8)
   a. Hold it.
   b. Keep it.
   c. Depend upon it.
5. Keep *track* of time (8)
   a. The train is on this *track*.
   b. We will *track* down the criminal.
   c. He lost *track* of his friend.

IV. Comprehension of Grammatical Structure

In the following paragraph fill each blank with a word which is suitable to the structure of the sentence and the sense of the passage. The words you supply will be structure words of some kind: prepositions, conjunctions, subordinators, etc. When you have finished, check with paragraph 2 of the narrative. Is your word in each case either the same as the word in the original or a suitable substitute for it in that it performs the same function?

Leadville is unique in being _____ highest city in the United States. It is located _____ the Rocky Mountains and is 10,000 feet above sea level. Its most unusual feature, _____, is the living picture of the past which it preserves. Leadville is not really old in years. It has existed less _____ a century, _____ it recalls an episode in the history of the West. _____ the town was in its heyday as late _____ 1890, it had a population of some 40,000 living in wooden houses _____ similar architecture, adorned _____ the wooden scrolls _____ ornamentation that were popular in _____ Victorian age in America. Now only 5000 live _____ and occupy the old houses. Many _____ the buildings are _____ disrepair and _____ need of paint, and _____ the town is close to the timberline, there is a certain bareness _____ its appearance apart _____ the drabness of its houses. Nevertheless, there is a romantic glamour there. The big hotel, _____ Tabor opera house, and even some of _____ notorious saloons are still used, and one can imagine _____ life was lived in the days _____ every citizen hoped _____ become a millionaire.

V. Comprehension of Main Ideas and Organizational Pattern

1. Language can be used for the practical concerns of life or it can be used to create art forms. Sometimes the dividing line between exposition (material designed primarily to inform) and narration (material designed primarily to entertain, such as the short story and the novel) is quite thin. This selection certainly contains elements of both. From the title, how did the authors view this selection—as one primarily to entertain or to inform?
2. If the narrative is the important feature of this selection, what purpose do the first two paragraphs serve?
3. This narrative presents an attitude toward the town and about the legend. What is this attitude? Where is it stated?
4. How does this simple narrative differ from a short story? How does it differ from a novel? Are there some elements of the short story and the novel in this selection?

VI. Composition

OF INTERMEDIATE DIFFICULTY

Write a paragraph developing one of the following topic sentences.
1. Horace A. W. Tabor was a person who was not afraid to take a chance.
2. Although Mr. Tabor spent some of his money on worthwhile projects, he spent much of it extravagantly.

ADVANCED

Write a paragraph developing one of the following topic sentences.
1. There are several lessons that can be learned from the story of Mr. Tabor.
2. The Rockefeller and Ford Foundations spend money much more wisely than Mr. Tabor spent his.

Essay 7
COVERED WAGON DAYS

Word Study

1. community /kəmyúnəti/
2. throng /θrɔŋ/
3. establish /əstǽblɪʃ/
4. resident /rézədənt/
5. yoke /yok/
6. utensil /yuténsəl/
7. lantern /lǽntərn/
8. jog /dʒɑg/
9. shallow /ʃǽlo/
10. rut /rət/
11. sod /sɑd/
12. hostile /hɑ́stəl/
13. agency /édʒənsi/
14. antelope /ǽntəlop/
15. duck /dək/
16. blizzard /blɪzərd/
17. biscuit /bískət/
18. venison /vénəsən/
19. squatter /skwɑ́tər/
20. stake /stek/
21. hardship /hɑ́rdʃɪp/

The words in the above list may need definition. Some of them are related to words you probably already know. Whenever they are, the related word is given in parentheses.

1. *community* a group of people living in the same area under the same laws (common)
2. *throng* a large crowd
3. *establish* begin, set up on a firm basis
4. *resident* a person who lives in a residence, or living place (residence)
5. *yoke* a piece of wood joining a team of animals
6. *utensil* an implement; a thing used to make something, as a cooking *utensil*
7. *lantern* A case for carrying a light. The case lets the light shine through it.
8. *jog* to move or travel with a jerking motion
9. *shallow* Not deep. The water in a river is *shallow* when there is little rain.
10. *rut* a deep mark in the road made by a wheel
11. *sod* Earth containing grass and roots. Pioneers lived in *sod* houses in areas where there were no trees.
12. *hostile* Unfriendly. An enemy is *hostile*.
13. *agency* An agent is a person who has charge of an area. The *agency* is the agent's office. (agent)

14. *antelope*   A small animal something like a deer. It is light brown with a white tail that stands straight up when it runs.
15. *duck*   To bend down or to go under something quickly. He *ducked* his head. The bad boy *ducked* under the bed.
16. *blizzard*   a severe wind and snow storm
17. *biscuit*   a sort of bread baked in the form of a small cake and usually served hot
18. *venison*   edible meat of deer, antelope, or elk
19. *squatter*   From the verb *squat*, meaning to sit down on one's heels. A *squatter* is a person who "sits down" on unoccupied land. On the American frontier, if the squatter was not disturbed for a certain length of time, he could claim the land by "squatter's rights."
20. *stake*   a piece of wood or metal pointed on one end for driving into the ground
21. *hardship*   Something that is hard or difficult. It is a *hardship* not to have enough to eat. It does not refer to *hard* as the opposite of *soft*. (hard)

Reading Suggestions
Like the previous selection, the one which follows is a narrative. Look for the cues that show the time sequence.

COVERED WAGON DAYS

1. The settlement of much of the territory west of the Mississippi River has taken place within the last one hundred years, within the memory of people now living. Rapid City, South Dakota, a fast-growing modern business center of some 60,000 people located at the eastern edge of the Black Hills, is a *community* (1) that has been settled in recent years. The Black Hills, a region of low, beautifully wooded mountains in the western part of the state, first became known in the 1870s when gold was discovered there. Most of the South Dakota territory belonged to the Indians at that time, but the white men soon came to the Rapid City area in *throngs* (2), some to search for gold and some to farm or *establish* (3) businesses for the new settlement.

2. Some years ago, the children of the third grade in one of the schools in Rapid City wrote to Mrs. Orpha Haxby, an 80-year-old *resident* (4) of the city, to ask her about her childhood experiences as a real pioneer. The following letter is her reply telling about her 300-mile trip by covered wagon from Elk Point, South Dakota, to Rapid City. This journey that took seven weeks in 1876 can now be made in one day by car or in one hour by airplane. You will note that

in writing to children she wrote from the child's point of view, emphasizing the excitement she felt as a child. She failed to mention, however, that the men were always conscious of the dangers involved and that the women were saddened by the breaking of home ties. Mrs. Haxby has said that her mother cried during the whole trip, feeling that she would never see her family again.

November 13, 1944
Rapid City, South Dakota

Dear Children:

3. Yes, I was a pioneer when I came with my father, mother, and two older sisters to the Black Hills of South Dakota.

We left Elk Point, South Dakota, in early October, 1876, in a covered wagon drawn by two *yoke* (5) of oxen, with a few necessary belongings: our clothing, bedding, dishes, cooking *utensils* (6), a kerosene *lantern* (7), a tent, camp stove, my mother's rocking chair, and, of course, food. I was allowed to bring my schoolbooks and a few toys. We also had six cows, a crate of chickens on the rear end of the wagon box, and one pony. We started with four cats, as my father had promised some of his friends he would bring them each a cat. Well, we arrived with only one—my pet. I shall always feel grateful to him, for he slept at my feet all the way and kept them warm. The cats and chickens soon learned that the wagon was their home. But the cats would go hunting at night, and at different times three failed to get back in the morning before we were ready to start and had to be left behind. The chickens were always turned loose when we first made camp in the evening, to stretch their wings and get exercise. They cackled and scratched around until dark and then flew into their box to sleep. The cattle were different. They had to be watched at night by a man called the night herder. He slept in the wagon during the day as we *jogged* (8) along.

5. After our tent was put up at night and a fire was going in the camp stove, we were comfortable, even though the snow sometimes had to be scraped away before putting up the tent. Many times I had to knock my feet together to keep them warm while waiting. After supper, we spread our beds on the ground.

6. Our food was cooked outside over an open fire. Our bread was baked in a Dutch oven, a heavy iron kettle with three short legs and a heavy iron lid with a rim about an inch high. The bread dough was patted out the size of the kettle and an inch thick. The oven was heated by placing it over a bed of hot coals, and more coals were placed on the lid, which shows the need of the rim to keep them from falling off. Some old-timers still say this is the best way to make bread, and it certainly is good.

7. Our food consisted mostly of bread, bacon, ham, beans, rice, dried fruits, tea, coffee, and sugar. We had milk from the cows, and the hens occasionally laid eggs. We could not have vegetables or canned goods because they would freeze.

8. We carried our wood tied under the wagon unless we were going to camp near a stream where there was timber.

9. We had only two real rivers to cross, the Missouri and the Cheyenne. When we reached the Missouri River at Pierre, the ice was not strong enough to carry the heavily loaded wagons, so we waited about a week for it to get thicker. Even then we were not allowed to ride. Instead, we walked alongside at a safe distance, and I could see cracks in the ice radiating in all directions. By the time the last wagon came along, the ice was so weakened that it broke through just as it reached the edge, but the teams were on the bank and pulled it through. At the Cheyenne River the ice was not safe either; but since it was a *shallow* (9) stream, a channel was cut through the ice wide enough for the wagons, and the river was forded.

10. As you know, an ox is a slow animal and when traveling day after day can only go 12 or 15 miles a day. That is why it took seven weeks to make a trip of around 300 miles. The riding was not very rough, as we traveled so slowly, although the road in some places was only a trail with deep *ruts* (10) made by other wagons when the ground was wet.

11. The first day we went only as far as Vermillion. The second day we got to Yankton, where we were to meet a large ox train from Sioux City. The train, which was loaded with freight for the Black Hills, was delayed. It was not safe for one wagon to go alone, so we joined another train of ten wagons, which was leaving at once. In the party were ten men, three women, and two children. All the men had guns for protection, in case we should be attacked by the Indians.

12. After we left the settlements above Yankton we saw no more houses, with one exception, until we came to Fort Thompson, an Indian agency. This exception was a lonely *sod* (11) house on the bare prairie that was occupied by a young man and his wife. We asked to go in and get warm at noon, for we made very short stops at that time, sometimes none at all, but we camped earlier at night. They were pleased to see us and treated us royally. They said they did not expect to see any more people until spring, as all their neighbors had gone away for the winter. They burned hay, which they twisted into hard rolls with their hands. They seemed to have little to eat but bread and some small potatoes they had raised and then placed in a hole in the dirt floor under the bed to keep them from freezing. The woman was so hungry for sugar that my mother gave her all she could spare from our supply. Their house was not as warm as our tent.

13. From Fort Thompson on, there were no more settlements until we reached a post office and store called Firesteel, which no longer exists, although the old store building still stands. We then traveled through an uninhabited country until we came to Pierre on the Missouri River. There were no settlements of white people from there to the Black Hills.

14. After we crossed the Missouri River we were on Indian land, but we did not see an Indian from there to Rapid City, a distance of nearly two hundred miles. They had been very *hostile* (12) throughout the summer but had now gone back to their *agencies* (13) for the winter. That is the reason we were traveling in cold weather. Along the road we saw several new graves of men who had been killed the previous summer.

15. We were now in a wild game country, but did not stop to hunt, although we saw bands of *antelope* (14). The lively little prairie dogs would sit up on the dirt mounds around their holes, jerk their little tails, and bark at us as we passed. My sister and I tried to catch some, but they always *ducked* (15) into their holes just as we got there.

16. Our first sight of the Black Hills was from Grindstone Butte, a high point about seventy-five miles from them. They were just a dim, dark blue outline against the sky. The color is due to the heavy pine trees on their surface. They looked beautiful, and I was not disappointed when we got closer and I could see what they looked like. Our last camp before reaching Rapid City was at a spring called Wasta, an Indian word meaning "good." That night there was a *blizzard* (16), the worst storm of the trip. The cattle got away, the tent blew down on us, and I was awakened by the snow blowing in my face. With the help of the night herder my father got the tent up, and we went to sleep again. The next day we reached Rapid City after dark. A man came to the creek with a lantern to show us across. My father's friends had a warm supper of hot baking-powder *biscuits* (17), *venison* (18) steak with gravy, and coffee ready for us. And was it good!

17. At first we lived in log houses with dirt floors and roofs made of poles, hay, and dirt. The roofs were fine unless it rained for several days until they were wet through, and then they did leak.

18. In the early days the land was claimed by what was called a "*squatter's* (19) right," by marking it out with *stakes* (20) at the corners, building a cabin, and living on it. It was the same with gold claims, except that one had to do a certain amount of mining work each year instead of living on them.

19. This is the story of my coming to the beautiful Black Hills, where I have since lived and hope to live for the rest of my life. There were *hardships* (21) and dangers, but something new and interesting

occurred every day, and I enjoyed every minute of the trip. (*1781 words*)

Most sincerely,
Orpha LeGro Haxby

EXERCISES

I. Comprehension of Details
To test your comprehension of the material you have just read, answer each of the following questions in a word or phrase.
1. How long does it now take to drive across the state of South Dakota by car from Elk Point to Rapid City?
2. How long did it take the covered wagon group to travel that same distance?
3. How were settlements protected in pioneer days?
4. Why did the group cross the state in the late autumn?
5. What animals did they take with them?
6. What animals did they see along the route?
7. How were the covered wagons pulled across the prairie?
8. Who enjoyed the trip more, the children or their mother?
9. Give three reasons why settlers came into the Black Hills region.
10. Why do many people go to the Black Hills now?

II. Skimming Exercise
As quickly as possible, find the number of the paragraph that gives you information about each of the following.
1. The kind of food the covered wagon group took with them
2. How the group baked their bread along the way
3. A description of the home of the settlers where the group stopped between Yankton and Fort Thompson
4. How the wagons crossed the two rivers they came to
5. What happened to the group at Wasta on the last night of their trip
6. How they were greeted when they got to Rapid City
7. The kind of house they lived in when they first arrived
8. How most of the land was claimed in the early days

III. Vocabulary Exercises

WORD STUDY

Choose from each of the following lists appropriate words to fill the blanks in the sentences that immediately follow.

1. *squatter, hostile, hardships, sod, ruts, blizzard*
   Mrs. Haxby went to Rapid City through _____ Indian country, and her group had many _____. The roads were rough because of the deep _____, and there was a bad _____ during which their tent blew down.

2. *agency, venison, jogged, utensils, antelope, throng, biscuits, lantern*
   They saw _____ as they _____ along the road. They carried a _____ so that they could see at night, and they had a few cooking _____. When they reached Rapid City, they ate _____ and _____.

3. *sod, establish, stake, community, agency*
   Mrs. Haxby's parents wanted to _____ residence in a new _____.

   The house would probably be made of _____.

WORDS WITH MULTIPLE MEANINGS

Circle the letter preceding the sentence in which the italicized word is used with a meaning close to that in the sentence taken from the narrative.

1. The chickens were always *turned* loose. (4)
   a. I hope the weather doesn't *turn* cold.
   b. His request was *turned* down.
   c. Many applicants for the position were *turned* away.

2. I had to knock my feet *together* to keep warm. (5)
   a. He put the broken pieces back *together*.
   b. We went *together* to the movie.
   c. This idea, *together* with others, is important.

3. We asked to go in and *get* warm. (12)
   a. I will *get* ready to go immediately.
   b. Let me *get* the book for you.
   c. We will soon *get* the tent up.

4. From Fort Thompson *on*, there were no more settlements. (13)
   a. The book is *on* the desk.
   b. Let's not stay here. Let's go *on*.
   c. He wanted to go *on* the stage.

5. The old building *still* stands. (13)
   a. He is here *still*. He has not left.
   b. Be *still* and listen to me.
   c. Try to stand *still* for a few minutes.

6. We were now in wild *game* territory. (15)
   a. The children were busy playing a *game*.
   b. Wild ducks are *game* birds in North America.
   c. Gamblers enjoy *games* of chance.

IV. Comprehension of Grammatical Structure

Answer the questions about these sentences from the essay. The numbers in parentheses indicate the paragraph from which the sentence is taken.

1. Rapid City, South Dakota, a fast-growing modern business center of some 60,000 people located at the eastern edge of the Black Hills, is a community that has been settled in recent years. (1)
   a. What is the subject of this sentence?
   b. What is the verb that goes with this subject?
   c. Find two structures that modify *Rapid City, South Dakota.*
   d. Find a structure that modifies *community.*
   e. What is the subject of *has been settled*?
   f. What is the meaning of *some* in *some* 60,000 people?

2. Most of the South Dakota territory belonged to the Indians at that time, but the white men soon came to Rapid City in throngs, some to search for gold and some to farm or establish businesses in the new settlement. (1)
   a. How many main sentence patterns are there in this sentence?
   b. What word joins the patterns?
   c. What does *some* in the expression *some to search* refer to?
   d. Is *some* used here in the same way as in Sentence 1 above?
   e. What infinitives tell the purpose for which the men came?

3. After our tent was put up at night and a fire was going in the camp stove, we were comfortable, even though the snow sometimes had to be scraped away before putting up the tent. (5)
   a. What is the main sentence pattern in this sentence?
   b. What subordinating patterns are there?
   c. What subordinating words join each of the patterns?
   d. What modifies *had to be scraped away*?
   e. What is the object of the preposition *before*?
   f. What two examples of the passive voice do you find in this sentence?

V. Comprehension of Main Ideas and Organizational Pattern

1. In what way is the purpose of this selection the same as that of the previous one? In what way is it different?
2. The first part of Mrs. Haxby's letter tells about what the group took with them and how they lived on the trip. The last part tells of the trip in chronological order. In what paragraph does the chronological account begin?
3. Paragraph 11 begins "The first day . . ." Paragraph 12 begins "After we left the settlements, . . ." What key words in the subsequent paragraphs show the time progression?
4. What is the function of paragraphs 17 and 18?
5. What is the function of the last paragraph?

VI. Composition

OF INTERMEDIATE DIFFICULTY

Write a paragraph developing one of the following topic sentences.
1. Life in a pioneer wagon train was full of new experiences for the children.
2. Pioneer trips to the West held many hardships for the women.
3. The men in a pioneer wagon train had to plan well to meet difficulties.

ADVANCED

Write a short essay on one of the following.
1. Character and Personality Traits That Would Be Valuable in a Pioneer
2. My Motives in Coming to the United States

Essay 8
AMERICAN SPORTS

Word Study

1. competitive /kəmpɛtətɪv/
2. spectator /spɛ́ktetər/
3. participant /pɑrtísɪpənt/
4. tournament /tə́rnəmənt/
5. professional /prəfɛ́ʃənəl/
6. alternate /ɔ́ltərnet/ (verb)
7. amateur /ǽmətyər/
8. championship /tʃǽmpiənʃɪp/
9. originate /ərídʒənet/
10. pad /pæd/
11. intricate /íntrəkət/
12. execute /ɛ́ksəkyut/
13. spectacularly /spɛktǽkyələrli/
14. gamble /gǽmbəl/
15. obstacle /ɑ́bstɪkəl/
16. fanatical /fənǽtɪkəl/
17. strenuous /strɛ́nyuəs/
18. vital /vaɪtəl/
19. existence /ɛgzístənts/
20. stock /stɑk/
21. inexhaustible /ɪnɪgzɔ́stəbəl/

Try to determine the meaning of these words from their use in the following sentences.

1. A *competitive* sport is one in which two or more people or teams try to see who can give the best performance.
2. Ten thousand *spectators* watched the ball game.
3. Julie is taking part in the game. She is a *participant*.
4. The teams play in a *tournament* to determine which team is the best.
5. A *professional* performance is one for which money is accepted. Members of a professional ball team get paid for playing.
6. The teams *alternate* the places where they play. They play in one town one week and the other town the next.
7. An *amateur* is one who takes part in a sport just for the joy of doing it. He is not paid for it.
8. A person who wins a tournament is a champion. The position he holds is the *championship*.
9. If a man starts a new custom or thinks up a new plan, he has *originated* it.
10. A wooden bench is softer to sit on after it is *padded* with soft material.
11. The Taj Mahal is noted for the *intricate* or detailed carving on its walls.
12. The skier *executed* his jump well. He performed it with skill.

13. If there is an unusual display of skill in a game, we call the game a spectacle, and we say that the players played *spectacularly*
14. If one takes a risk in order to gain an advantage, he is *gambling*.
15. The big stones in our path were *obstacles* to our running.
16. If a person pursues an activity beyond the bounds of good sense, we say he is *fanatical*.
17. Running fast is *strenuous* exercise.
18. A man's heartbeat is *vital* to his life. He would die without it.
19. Many men believe in the *existence* of God. They believe that God lives.
20. The merchant's shelves are well *stocked*. He had a lot of things for sale.
21. He worked night and day and always seemed to have a great deal of energy left. His energy seemed *inexhaustible*.

Reading Suggestions
This essay is organized by topics, or by division into two sections: spectator sports and participant sports. As you read, look for this division and for the kinds of sports that are discussed in each section.

AMERICAN SPORTS

1. The United States is a sports-loving nation. Sports in America take a variety of forms; organized *competitive* (1) struggles, which draw huge crowds to cheer their favorite team to victory; athletic games, played for recreation anywhere sufficient space is found; and hunting and fishing. Most sports are seasonal, so that what is happening in sports depends upon the time of year. Some sports are called *spectator* (2) sports, as the number of spectators greatly exceeds the number playing in the game. Other sports are called *participant* (3) sports, drawing a crowd of onlookers only on special occasions, such as *tournaments* (4). Some sports are commercial and *professional* (5), with players who are paid for their participation and with audiences who pay admission to watch.

2. Baseball is the most popular sport in the United States. It is played throughout the spring and summer, and professional baseball teams play well into the fall. Although no other game is exactly like baseball, perhaps the one most nearly like it is the English game of cricket. In baseball there are nine men on each side. The two teams *alternate* (6) at the bat (the offense) and in the field (the defense). Each pair of turns at bat is called an inning. There are nine innings in a game. Not only is baseball played by boys in their neighborhoods and by high school and college teams in the spring, but it is also played by grown men as *amateurs* (7) and as professionals organized into major and minor leagues. On a fine summer evening after dinner,

there are probably more than twenty thousand games of baseball being played throughout the country. Every fall there is the World Series, a play-off for the professional *championship* (8) between the top two teams of the nation — one the winner of the National League competition and the other of the American League. Heroes in baseball are talked about and remembered as in perhaps no other sport. Every schoolboy looks up to Babe Ruth, Joe Dimaggio, Dizzy Dean, and Jackie Robinson, among others.

3. Football is the most popular sport in the fall. The game *originated* (9) as a college sport more than seventy-five years ago. It is still played by almost every college and university in the country, and the football stadiums of some of the largest universities seat as many as eighty thousand people. The game is not the same as European football or soccer. In American football there are eleven players on each team, and they are dressed in *padded* (10) uniforms and helmets because the game is rough and injuries are likely to occur. The object of the game is to carry or forward pass (that is, throw from one person to another) the football across the opponent's goal, or scoring line. The team with the ball has four chances, called "downs," to gain a minimum of 10 yards. If the team is unsuccessful, the ball is turned over to the opposing team, which has four chances to advance the ball the minimum 10-yard distance. He who has not attended a large college football game has missed one of the most colorful aspects of American college life. Between the two halves of the game, the playing field is taken over by the bands of the rival institutions, which take turns doing *intricate* (11) marches and *executing* (12) interesting formations. The student spectators are led in cheering for their teams by trained, uniformed student cheerleaders, many of whom are pretty girls. Outstanding high school football players are usually encouraged to come to a college or university by offers of scholarships and free room and board. Football is so popular, and the urge to win is so keen, that many colleges actively seek outstanding players for their student body. Attendance at football games is so large that it is not unheard of for a college or university to finance its entire athletic program from ticket sales.

4. There are professional football teams in nearly all major cities of the United States. Their players are almost always former college football players. The number of spectators at professional football games is larger than at college games, because the professional players, quite naturally, are more skilled and perform more *spectacularly* (13). Whereas college football games are usually played on Saturday afternoons, professional football games are customarily played on Sunday afternoons or evenings.

5. Basketball is the winter sport in American schools and colleges. Like football, basketball originated in the United States and is not

yet popular in other countries. Many Americans prefer it to football because it is played indoors throughout the winter and because it is a faster game. It is a very popular game with high schools, and in more than twenty states, state-wide high school tournaments are held yearly. Professional basketball teams exist, but they do not attract as many fans as professional baseball teams do.

6. Other spectator sports include wrestling, boxing, and horse racing. Although horse-racing fans call themselves sportsmen, the accuracy of the term is questionable, as only the jockeys who ride the horses in the races can be considered athletes. The so-called sportsmen are the spectators, who do not assemble primarily to see the horses race, but to bet upon the outcome of each race. *Gambling* (14) is the attraction of horse racing.

7. There are many participant sports in America. Golf is probably the most popular. Although the game originated in Scotland, it is possibly more popular in the United States than anywhere else. It is played whenever weather permits. Frozen ground and snow are the only *obstacles* (15) that will stop *fanatical* (16) golfers from playing. There are now more golfers than tennis players, and this fact probably explains why the United States is no longer producing tennis teams of the caliber it once did.

8. Swimming, water skiing, and skin diving are very popular summer sports. In the winter, ice skating, skiing, and hockey are the fashion.

9. In recent years there has been a great increase in the popularity of indoor bowling. Most bowling alleys are operated as private businesses, and bowling is carried on throughout the fall, winter, and spring. Bowling is a popular sport with young and old. It is easily played and is enjoyed by persons who have grown too old to care for more *strenuous* (17) athletic activities.

10. A person cannot truly understand the role of sports in American life, however, if he does not understand how very much most American men like to hunt and fish. Skill in these activities was once *vital* (18) to frontier *existence* (19). Even though it is no longer necessary to kill wild game or catch fish in order to live, the devotion to these activities has remained. In order to keep a plentiful supply of wild game, the state governments forbid the hunting of certain animals and birds except during stated weeks in the year, called "seasons." Thus there is a duck season, a deer season, and so forth, each of which lasts for several weeks. Hunters have to purchase licenses to hunt, and the laws limit the number of animals or birds a hunter may secure in one day or season. Deep-sea fishing is popular along the seacoasts. Inland there are thousands of lakes, particularly in Minnesota and Wisconsin, and numerous rivers and streams in which one may fish. Many streams and lakes are *stocked* (20) with young fish

from state fish hatcheries. Often a boy and his father will get into the family car and head for their favorite fishing spot when the day is over. Much hunting and fishing is still done in almost uninhabited country which must be reached by small boats, by hiking through woods, or sometimes by horseback or hydroplanes.

11. Boys play many games that men do, particularly baseball, basketball, and football. There are some sports, however, that are played only by children. The most popular one for boys is marbles, which is played mainly in the spring. For girls there is hopscotch and jacks. Children of both sexes play hide-and-seek, tag, and kick-the-can. They also swing and teeter-totter.

12. But as much as Americans like to engage in sports or to watch games being played, they seem to have fully as much fun reading and talking about sports. Usually, several pages of the daily paper are devoted to discussing sports events, and games are carried on television and radio. In almost any social gathering, people get around to talking about such things as outstanding players and games of former years, the current prospects for teams in the season ahead, which team is going to win the championship, what kind of fishing rod or gun to buy, or what records are most likely to be broken. The subject of sports is as *inexhaustible* (21) as the enthusiasm of its lovers. (*1469 words*)

EXERCISES

I. Comprehension of Details
Indicate whether each of the following statements is true or false by writing the letter T or F in the space provided.

_____ 1. In America, football and baseball, rather than a large variety of sports, tend to be popular.

_____ 2. Spectator sports are those in which the spectators take part.

_____ 3. Baseball is something like the English game of cricket.

_____ 4. The World Series is a play-off of amateur baseball teams.

_____ 5. Baseball is a popular game in the spring.

_____ 6. Baseball is a game primarily for children.

_____ 7. Football is the most popular sport in America.

_____ 8. Attendance at college football games is so large that sometimes colleges are able to finance their entire athletic program from football ticket sales.

_____ 9. Golf is one of the most popular participant sports.

_____ 10. College football players are considered professionals.

_____ 11. Football may be classified as a spectator sport.

_____ 12. American football is the same as European soccer.

_____ 13. Volleyball is the winter sport in American high schools and colleges.

_____ 14. Outdoor bowling is very popular in America.

_____ 15. There is no longer a plentiful supply of wild game to make hunting popular in America.

_____ 16. Wild game can be hunted all year long in the United States.

_____ 17. Horse racing is not popular in the United States.

_____ 18. Much hunting and fishing in America is still done in almost uninhabited country.

_____ 19. All lakes and streams in America have a plentiful natural supply of fish.

_____ 20. Many Americans seem to have fully as much fun reading and talking about sports as engaging in them or watching games being played.

II. Skimming Exercise
As quickly as possible, find the number of the paragraph where each of the topics in exercise I is mentioned or discussed.

III. Vocabulary Exercises

WORD STUDY

In the following paragraph draw a line through the word in parentheses that does not complete the sentence meaningfully.

I like to play golf, but with me it is just a hobby. I am not (a professional, an amateur). Furthermore, I am not good at the game, and during tournaments I am just a (participant, spectator). I never hope to win (a tournament, an obstacle). My elderly uncle says he likes golf because it is not too (fanatical, strenuous) a game. He has played a long time and says that golf (originated, padded) in Scotland. He has almost (inexhaustible, intricate) knowledge of the lives of the great golfers of our time. Each week we (alternate, originate) taking each other to the country club to play on Sunday mornings.

WORDS WITH MULTIPLE MEANINGS

In each of the following, circle the letter preceding the phrase or sentence that best illustrates the meaning of the italicized words. Numbers in parentheses refer to the paragraphs in which the words occur.

1. Professional baseball teams play *well* into the fall. (2)
   a. The playing in the fall is good.
   b. They play late in the fall.
   c. They certainly play in the fall.

2. Every year there is the World Series, a *play-off* for the professional championship. (2)
   a. a final play
   b. a contest
   c. a series of plays
3. The ball is *turned over* to the opposing team. (3)
   a. given to the opposing team
   b. rolled across the field to the opposing team
   c. turned over on the other side
4. The playing field is *taken over* by the bands of the rival institutions. (3)
   a. used only by
   b. captured by
   c. operated by
5. The bands *take turns* doing intricate marches. (3)
   a. alternate
   b. go in a circle
   c. turn around

IV. Comprehension of Grammatical Structure

EXERCISE A

Supply the missing words in the following paragraphs. Do not look at the essay. When you have finished, check with paragraph 12 of the essay.

But as much as Americans _____ to engage in sports or to _____ games being played, they seem _____ have fully as much fun reading _____ talking about sports. Usually, several _____ of the daily paper are devoted _____ discussing sports events, and games _____ carried on television and radio. _____ almost any social gathering, people _____ around to talking about such _____ as outstanding players and games _____ former years, the current prospects _____ teams in the season ahead, _____ team is going to win _____ championship, what kind of fishing _____ or gun to buy, or _____ records are most likely to _____ broken. The subject of sports _____ as inexhaustible as the enthusiasm _____ its lovers.

EXERCISE B

To test your comprehension of sentence structure and improve your ability to handle it, combine each of the following groups of sentences into one sentence following the suggestions given and eliminating unnecessary words. Then find that structure or a similar one in the essay.

1. Sports in America take a variety of forms. There are organized competitive struggles. These draw large crowds. There are athletic games. People play these for recreation. (Use *such as* and *which*.)
2. No other game is exactly like baseball. One is most nearly like it. This is cricket. (Use *but*).
3. Attendance at football games is large. A college or university can finance its entire athletic program from ticket sales. (Use *so . . . that*.)
4. The number of spectators at college football games is large. The number of spectators at professional football games is larger. The professional players are more skilled. They perform more spectacularly. (Use *but* and *and*.)

V. Comprehension of Main Ideas and Organizational Pattern

Answer orally the following questions about the organizational pattern of the selection.

1. What is the subject of paragraph 2? Why do you think the author mentioned this subject first?
2. What words in the opening sentence of paragraph 3 relate it to the topic of paragraph 2?
3. In what way is paragraph 4 related to paragraph 3?
4. In what way does paragraph 5 follow the plan of paragraphs 2 and 3?
5. What transitional words in the first sentence of paragraph 6 relate it to the preceding paragraphs?
6. In what way does the topic of paragraph 7 differ from the topics of paragraphs 2 through 6?
7. How are the topics of paragraphs 8, 9, and 10 similar to that of paragraph 7?
8. Is any new aspect of sports in America introduced in paragraph 12?
9. What is the function of paragraph 1 in relation to the essay as a whole? Of paragraph 12?
10. If you were to divide the article into two parts, where would the division come?

VI. Composition

OF INTERMEDIATE DIFFICULTY

Write a paragraph developing one of the following topic sentences.

1. The United States has different types of sports at different seasons of the year.
2. There are many participant sports in the United States.
3. Boys in the United States play many of the games that men do.

ADVANCED

Write a paragraph developing one of the following topic sentences.
1. I would rather watch a football game than play in one.
2. _____ is my favorite summer sport.
3. The most unusual sport in my country is _____.

Essay 9

THE AMERICAN ATTITUDE TOWARD MANUAL LABOR

Word Study

1. glorification /glɔrɪfɪkéʃən/
2. wilderness /wíldərnəs/
3. manual /mǽnyuəl/
4. genuine /dʒɛ́nyuən/
5. hobby /hábɪ/
6. militant /mílətənt/
7. carpentry /kárpəntri/
8. welding /wéldɪŋ/
9. bricklayer /bríkleər/
10. compensate /kámpənset/
11. prestige /prɛstíʒ/
12. stenographer /stənágrəfər/
13. upholstering /əphólstərɪŋ/
14. project /prádʒɛkt/
15. exhibit /ɛgzíbət/

Words related to words you may already know:
1. *glorification* glory
2. *wilderness* wild
3. *manual* hand (from Latin *manus*)
6. *militant* military
9. *bricklayer* brick

Words that may need definition:
4. *genuine* real
5. *hobby* something a person likes to do for entertainment in his leisure time
7. *carpentry* work done by a carpenter, one who builds and repairs things made of wood, such as houses and furniture
8. *welding* the process of uniting two metal objects by hammering or pressing them together after they have been softened by heat
10. *compensate* to give something in payment for a loss or damage
11. *prestige* the power to demand admiration or esteem because of great achievement
12. *stenographer* a person who types material usually written in shorthand from dictation by another person
13. *upholstering* covering furniture with padding and fabric for purposes of decoration and comfort
14. *project* an undertaking; a plan of action
15. *exhibit* to show to others

Reading Suggestions

The purpose of this essay is to explain the American attitude toward manual labor. As you read, look for the sentence in the introduction (the first two paragraphs) that states what this attitude is. This essay has cause and effect organization. It tells first how an attitude has developed (paragraphs 1 and 2) and then what the effects of this attitude on American society have been.

THE AMERICAN ATTITUDE TOWARD MANUAL LABOR

1. A characteristic of American culture that has become almost a tradition is the *glorification* (1) of the self-made man—the man who has risen to the top through his own efforts, usually beginning by working with his hands. While the leader in business or industry or the college professor occupies a higher social position and commands greater respect in the community than the common laborer or even the skilled factory worker, he may take pains to point out that his father started life in America as a farm hand or laborer of some sort.

2. Most of the people who settled the United States were poor. The country they came to was a *wilderness* (2). Land had to be cleared of trees in order to make farms; mines had to be developed; houses, shops, and public buildings had to be built. Everyone had to help build them. *Manual* (3) labor was highly valued. Later it was the man who worked with his head to achieve success in business and industry who was looked up to. Now there is in America a curious combination of pride in having risen to a position where it is no longer necessary to depend upon manual labor for a living and *genuine* (4) delight in what one is able to accomplish with his hands.

3. This attitude toward manual labor is seen in many aspects of American life. One is invited to dinner at a home that is not only comfortably but even luxuriously furnished, and in which there is every evidence of the fact that the family has been able to afford foreign travel, expensive *hobbies* (5), and college educations for the children; yet the hostess probably will cook the dinner herself, will serve it herself, and will wash the dishes afterward. Furthermore, the dinner will not consist merely of something quickly and easily assembled from the contents of various cans and a cake or pie bought at the nearby bakery. On the contrary, the hostess usually takes pride in careful preparation of special dishes. In addition, she does most of her other household work; and even though her husband may be a professional man, he talks about washing the car, digging in his flower beds, painting the house, or laying tile on the floor of the recreation room in the basement. His wife may even help him with these things, just as he often helps her with the dishwashing. The son who is away at college may wait on tables and wash dishes in a sorority

house for his board, or during the summer he may work with a construction gang on a new highway in order to earn his next year's school expenses.

4. Those who earn their living through manual labor command good salaries. *Militant* (6) labor unions have demanded and gotten high wages for workers in skilled trades such as *carpentry* (7), *welding* (8), and various kinds of factory work. Thus the standard of living for these workers is high. The *bricklayer* (9) probably earns more money than his neighbor who is a college professor. The white-collar workers, who may remain lower on the economic scale, are *compensated* (10) by the higher *prestige* (11) their positions often give them.

5. It has been an American ideal to rise from a humble beginning to a better position. Therefore the "servant class" has not remained a fixed group. In recent years it has almost ceased to exist because people who were once servants can get higher wages working in factories. The majority of families cannot afford to pay what people who do housework or gardening charge for their services. Girls who do housework by the hour sometimes make nearly as much as *stenographers* (12) or even public schoolteachers, providing they work the same number of hours. In a society that stresses equality, they do not wish to be treated as maids. In the homes of wealthy people, a woman who does housework may have a private apartment in the home and a liberal amount of free time. At one time, the South, where black help was more common, was an exception, but the South of today is following the pattern of the rest of the country, as all elements of society strive for equal treatment.

6. The expense of maid service and of skilled labor, such as painting and carpentry, and the tradition of working with one's hands have contributed to keeping alive the spirit of "do-it-yourself." Large sections of popular magazines are devoted to giving instructions in gardening, carpentry, *upholstering* (13), and interior decorating. Night school courses at the local high school teach Mrs. America how to sew her clothes and Mr. America how to grease his own car. The average American gets a great deal of pleasure out of telling others about his *projects* (14), *exhibiting* (15) them for his neighbors, or taking them to the county fair, where he is sure they will win a prize.

7. Foreigners sometimes draw the conclusion that an American is wealthier than he is because he has such things as a private motorboat or a beautifully landscaped garden. Yet they do not always realize that the American has these things only because he has made them himself. (*858 words*)

EXERCISES

I. Comprehension of Details

Choose the sentence fragment that best completes each of the following.

1. In America the person who commands a position of respect in the community
   a. generally finds it painful to admit that his father started life in America as a common laborer or farmhand.
   b. may be proud of the fact that his father was a common laborer or farmhand.
   c. is generally the son or grandson of a common laborer or farmhand.
   d. has generally risen to the top by working with his own hands.

2. The American attitude toward manual labor developed because
   a. it was the man who worked with his head to achieve success in business and industry who was looked up to.
   b. most of the people who originally came to America were poor.
   c. although manual labor was highly valued in building America in its early days, later success in industry came to the man who worked with his head.
   d. there is a curious sense of pride in having risen to a position where it is no longer necessary to depend upon manual labor for a living.

3. According to the essay, a woman whose husband earns a good salary may invite guests to a dinner she has cooked herself, mainly because
   a. servants in America are impossible to get.
   b. she takes pride in what she can do herself.
   c. she can't afford servants.
   d. it is easy to get a meal from cans or to buy things ready-made at the bakery.

4. The main point made about the salaries of those who do manual labor is that
   a. their high salaries do not give them social prestige equal to that of white-collar workers.
   b. they may enjoy a standard of living equal to that of many white-collar workers.
   c. because of militant labor unions they probably earn more than white-collar workers.
   d. they enjoy social prestige equal to that of white-collar workers because of the American glorification of manual labor.

5. The "servant class" in America has almost ceased to exist because
   a. mechanical gadgets do the jobs that servants used to do.

    b. the majority of families cannot afford to pay what people who do housework or gardening charge for their services.

    c. people who were once servants can get higher wages working in factories.

    d. in a society that stresses equality people do not want to be treated as servants.

6. According to the authors, the spirit of "do-it-yourself" in America

    a. is nourished by both the expense of skilled labor and the American tradition of manual labor.

    b. is now mainly a fad kept alive by popular magazines.

    c. has nearly died out owing to increased mechanization.

    d. is largely a matter of necessity.

II. Skimming Exercise

As quickly as possible, find the sentence in the essay which answers each of the questions in exercise I.

III. Vocabulary Exercises

WORD STUDY

The man who does bricklaying is called a bricklayer. In the blanks below write the word for the person who does each of the following types of work. (Use the -er suffix.) Then explain in your own words what each person does.

1. carpentry _____   3. upholstering _____

2. welding _____   4. stenography _____

WORDS WITH MULTIPLE MEANINGS

Circle the letter preceding the word or phrase that most closely expresses the meaning of each of the following expressions from the selection. Numbers in parentheses refer to paragraphs in the selection.

1. risen to the top (1)

    a. achieved great wealth

    b. chosen a respected profession

    c. became successful in his business or profession

    d. earned the affection of his associates

2. take pains (1)

    a. feel bad

    b. make a point

    c. be careful

    d. pay attention

3. looked up to (2)
   a. respected
   b. observed from below
   c. checked in a dictionary
   d. revered
4. on the contrary (3)
   a. but
   b. however
   c. moreover
   d. instead
5. providing (5)
   a. if
   b. because
   c. for
   d. and

IV. Comprehension of Grammatical Structure

Supply the missing words in the following paragraph. Do not look
at the selection.

Most of the people who _____ the United States were poor.
_____ country they came to was _____ wilderness. Land had to
be _____ of trees in order to _____ farms; mines had to be
_____; houses, shops, and public buildings _____ to be built.
Everyone had to help _____ them. Manual labor was highly
_____. Later it was the man _____ worked with his head to
achieve _____ in business and industry who _____ looked up to.
Now there _____ in America a curious combination _____ pride
in having risen to _____ position where it is no _____ necessary
to depend upon manual labor _____ a living and genuine delight
_____ what one is able to _____ with his hands.

Now turn back to page 76 and compare your paragraph with the
original version. If in each case you have not supplied the same
word, does your word belong to the same class of words (noun, adjective, verb, preposition, etc.)? Be prepared to explain why a word of
this particular class is necessary in each case. What are the cues in
the sentence structure that indicate it?

V. Comprehension of Main Ideas and Organizational Pattern

1. Find the sentence in the selection that best states what the American attitude toward manual labor is.
2. The topic sentence or statement of the central idea of paragraph 3
   is the first sentence. What do the words "This attitude" refer to?
   The words "many aspects of American life" give you a key as to
   what to expect in the rest of the paragraph. What group of people is discussed in this paragraph?

3. Paragraph 4 continues to develop the central idea of paragraph 3 by telling how the American attitude toward manual labor has affected another group of people. What group is discussed and what attitude is brought out?
4. What group of people is the subject of paragraph 5 and what attitude is illustrated?
5. What is the purpose of paragraph 6? How does it differ from the purpose of paragraphs 3, 4, and 5?

VI. Composition

EXERCISE A

Write a paragraph developing one of the following topic sentences.
1. The American attitude toward manual labor has developed because of the history of the country.
2. In an American household a family with a good income typically do many things for themselves.
3. The tradition of "do-it-yourself" is popular in America.

EXERCISE B

Write a paragraph developing one of the following topic sentences. To write on one of these, you will have to depart further from ideas in the text than in any of the previous assignments. All the sentences in your paragraph must support the central idea. To support statement 1 or 3, you must explain your reasons for liking or not liking the activity under discussion.
1. I do not like the American custom of the man helping with the dishes.
2. Servants are very nice to have.
3. I like to raise flowers (cook, do metalwork, paint, carve wood, repair old clocks, make pottery, etc.).

EXERCISE C

Write a short composition of three or four paragraphs on one of the following topics. For example, for topic 1 you might develop in each paragraph one reason why that particular servant was good by giving an example of something he or she did or a quality he or she possessed. Each paragraph might deal with one activity the servant carried on, or might list things he or she did for some member of the family. In topic 2 one or two paragraphs could develop the advantages, and one or two paragraphs could develop the disadvantages.
1. The Best Servant My Family Ever Had
2. The Advantages and Disadvantages of Making a Living by Brain Work
3. Differences in Attitudes Toward Servants in the United States and in My Native Country
4. Desirable (Undesirable) Aspects of Being a House Servant

THE AMERICAN CONCEPTION OF A HERO

Word Study

1. admiration /ædməréʃən/
2. observation /ɑbzərvéʃən/
3. adoration /ædəréʃən/
4. tolerate /tɑ́ləret/
5. humiliate /hyumíliet/
6. disagree /dɪsəgrí/
7. discourtesy /dɪskɔ́rtəsi/
8. unbelievable /ənbəlívəbəl/
9. unparalleled /ənpérələld/
10. humble /həmbəl/
11. eventually /ivéntʃuəlɪ/
12. secede /sisíd/
13. infinite /ínfənət/
14. opponent /əpónənt/
15. malice /mǽləs/
16. inaugural /ɪnɔ́gyərəl/
17. charity /tʃérəti/
18. vindictiveness /vɪndíktɪvnəs/
19. generosity /dʒɛnərásətɪ/
20. hysterical /hɪstérɪkəl/
21. funeral /fyúnərəl/
22. casket /kǽskət/
23. mourning /mɔ́rnɪŋ/
24. vengeance /véndʒənts/
25. martyr /mɑ́rtər/
26. criticism /krítəsɪzm/
27. tarnish /tɑ́rnɪʃ/
28. assassin /əsǽsən/

Words with common prefixes or suffixes (related words are given in parentheses):

-*ation*   noun ending meaning "act of"
1. *admiration*   act of feeling wonder or pleasure (admire, admirable)
2. *observation*   act of looking at something carefully (observe, observable)
3. *adoration*   act of worshiping or loving (adore, adorable)

-*ate*   verb ending
4. *tolerate*   to allow a condition to exist (toleration, tolerance)
5. *humiliate*   to make someone feel in an inferior position (humiliation)

dis-   prefix meaning "lack of"
6. *disagree*   to have a difference of opinion (agree, agreement, disagreement)
7. *discourtesy*   a lack of politeness (courtesy, courteous, discourteous)

un-   prefix meaning "not"
8. *unbelievable*   not believable (believable)
9. *unparalleled*   not running in the same direction (parallel)

Other words that may need definition:
10. *humble*   of low position
11. *eventually*   finally; in the end
12. *secede*   to withdraw from
13. *infinite*   without end; beyond measure or comprehension, as *infinite* space or God's *infinite* goodness
14. *opponent*   one on the opposite side, as an *opponent* in a game or argument
15. *malice*   desire to harm another person
16. *inaugural*   of an inauguration, or beginning, of something. When the president of the United States takes office, there is an *inaugural* ceremony in which he makes a speech.
17. *charity*   act of good will or affection
18. *vindictiveness*   wanting to repay someone for a wrong he has done one
19. *generosity*   wanting to give or share
20. *hysterical*   emotionally uncontrolled
21. *funeral*   a ceremony for the dead
22. *casket*   a box in which a dead person is buried
23. *mourning*   feeling grief or sadness
24. *vengeance*   repayment for an injury done to one
25. *martyr*   one who is punished or killed for his beliefs
26. *criticism*   disapproval; finding fault
27. *tarnish*   to make a metal object dull which has been bright
28. *assassin*   a person who kills another

Reading Suggestions
After you have read this essay, you will be asked to analyze its plan of organization. As you read it, look for the statement of the central idea in the introductory paragraph. The last sentence of this paragraph indicates that the author will list qualities of the hero that Lincoln possessed. Look for the cue words at the beginning of the paragraphs that point out each new quality to be discussed.

THE AMERICAN CONCEPTION OF A HERO

1. Of all figures from America's past Abraham Lincoln is dearest to the hearts of the American people. In fact, the *admiration* (1) they have had for him borders on worship. Writers note the fact that the Lincoln Memorial in Washington, D.C., is not unlike the temples that ancient Greeks built in honor of their gods, and that the annual cere-

mony of celebrating Lincoln's birthday in schools and other public places has sometimes had characteristics of a religious service. Whether this last *observation* (2) is true or not, certainly Lincoln is a national hero. He had many of the qualities of the hero that have appealed to Americans.

2. First of all, Lincoln's career fits a popular American belief that every boy can dream of becoming president. In other words, no matter how *humble* (10) a person's beginning, there is no class system that prevents him from becoming a leader in industry, government, or any of the professions if he has ambition, brains, and a willingness to work. Americans admire the self-made man — the man who, with neither money nor family influence, fights his way to the top. Lincoln was born of poor parents. His mother died when he was young. The shack in which he and his father lived one winter had only three walls; the fourth side was open to the weather. He had little opportunity for schooling. Most of his early study was done by himself at night by the light of a fireplace. He did hard manual labor through the day — splitting rails for fences, taking care of livestock, working on a riverboat or in a store. But as he grew older he studied law in his spare time and set up a practice. He was a good speaker and student of political philosophy. His ability finally made a name for him, and *eventually* (11) he became president of the United States.

3. Lincoln is also admired because of his leadership during the difficult period of the Civil War. He dared to do what he thought was right at a time when his beliefs were unpopular with many people. He, in a sense, represents the spirit of union among the states. Before the Civil War, the economy of the South depended upon the plantation system which made use of slave labor. Reformers in the northern states put so much pressure upon the southerners to free their slaves that some of the southern states wanted to *secede* (12) from the United States. They argued that the question of slavery was a matter for the individual states to decide rather than the federal government, and they did not want to submit to its decision. The national government in Washington said that no state had the right to secede, and the Civil War was the result. If the South had won the war, what is now the United States might well have been divided into several countries with peculiar regional interests and problems. Lincoln dedicated himself to preserving the Union, and the northern states with him at their head were victorious. Americans from both the North and the South now generally feel that keeping the states together as one country has produced long-range benefits, and Lincoln has received much of the credit for holding the Union together.

4. Furthermore, Lincoln had many personal qualities that made him dear to the hearts of his countrymen. He had *infinite* (13) patience

and tolerance for those who *disagreed* (6) with him. As president, he appointed men to his cabinet whom he considered most capable for the job, even though some of them openly scorned him and *humiliated* (5) him. He bore their *discourtesy* (7) toward him with admirable restraint. He was generous to his *opponents* (14). There are many stories about his courteous treatment of southern leaders. When the war was over, he bore the South no *malice* (15). In his famous Second *Inaugural* (16) Address, the words of which are carved on the walls of the Lincoln Memorial, he said "With malice toward none, with *charity* (17) for all, with firmness in the right as God gives us to see the right, let us strive on to finish the work we are in, to bind up the nation's wounds, care for him who shall have borne the battle and for his widow and his orphan." Americans believe that if he had lived, he would not have *tolerated* (4) the *vindictiveness* (18) that crept into the northern plans for postwar government of the rebel states. Since *generosity* (19) toward a defeated opponent is admired by Americans, Lincoln fitted the national ideal of what is right.

5. Shortly after the Civil War was over, Lincoln was shot one night while attending a play in a Washington theater. He died within a few hours. The *hysterical* (20) reaction of the nation to his death was almost *unbelievable* (8) and demonstrated the *adoration* (3) in which he was held. Newspapers were edged with black; ministers gave praises of Lincoln instead of their prepared sermons. His *funeral* (21) procession in Washington was miles long. Lincoln's body was taken by train back to his former home in Springfield, Illinois, but in all the major cities through which the train passed, the *casket* (22) was paraded through streets lined with *mourning* (23) thousands. In the small towns through which the train passed, bells rang in honor of the dead president. Adoring citizens lit torches along the railroad track to show their last respects. It took the train twelve days to reach Springfield. Meanwhile, the hysterical demand for *vengeance* (24) upon Lincoln's *assassin* (28) was *unparalleled* (9) in United States history.

6. Thus the circumstances of his death made him a *martyr* (25) for a cause about which people were already highly emotional. This fact immediately set Lincoln apart in a spectacular way from other national heroes as did the recent deaths of John and Robert Kennedy. Had Lincoln lived, it might well be that his postwar policies would have brought *criticism* (26) upon him which would have *tarnished* (27) his popularity. Instead, an assassin's bullet erased in the minds of Americans any faults he had and emphasized his virtues. (*999 words*)

EXERCISES

I. Comprehension of Details

Indicate whether each of the following statements is true or false by writing the letter T or F in the space provided.

_____ 1. The Lincoln Memorial in Washington is a place of religious worship.

_____ 2. Abraham Lincoln went to a university to study law.

_____ 3. At the time Lincoln was president of the United States many of his beliefs were unpopular with many people.

_____ 4. Lincoln appointed men to be his advisers according to their capabilities and regardless of their feeling toward him.

_____ 5. The people in the South of the United States still generally feel that the outcome of the Civil War has had few benefits for them.

_____ 6. After Lincoln's death the North's postwar plans for governing the rebel states were not always wise.

_____ 7. Lincoln was a self-made man.

_____ 8. Lincoln's postwar policies brought criticism on him.

_____ 9. The question of rights of the individual states as opposed to the rights of the federal government was one of the issues in the American Civil War.

_____ 10. A major reason the southern states wanted to secede from the United States was the agricultural system on which their economy was based.

II. Skimming Exercise

When you have determined an author's central idea and have noted what his plan of organization will be, you can skim the article quickly for its main points by noting the topic sentences of the paragraphs that carry out this plan. For example, in the introduction to this essay the authors have told you they will develop their thesis sentence by showing you that the reasons for the veneration of Lincoln can perhaps be found in the fact that Lincoln had many of the qualities of the hero as conceived by Americans. If you look at the first sentence of nearly every paragraph, you will find one of those qualities stated. You can spot the qualities quickly by looking for the cue words (*first of all, also, furthermore*) that point to them. When you know what idea the paragraph will discuss, you can read more rapidly over the rest of the paragraph that describes the quality in more detail. This technique of looking for the main point at the beginning of a paragraph and then skimming the rest of the paragraph may help you to cover your textbook material more rapidly.

III. Vocabulary Exercises

WORD STUDY
List all the words you know that are related to each of the following
words, and tell whether each is a noun, verb, adjective, or adverb.

Tolerable — *toleration* (noun), *tolerance* (noun), *tolerate* (verb)

1. adorable   3. admiration
2. believe   4. disagreeable

Form nouns from the following verbs by adding the ending -*ation*.

Humiliate — *humiliation*

1. dedicate   3. assassinate
2. inaugurate   4. admire

Make the following adjectives negative by adding the prefix *un-*

1. tarnished   3. charitable
2. restrained   4. observable

Use the following words in sentences to show that you know their
meaning.

1. eventually   5. admiration   8. disagree
2. criticism   6. vengeance   9. tarnish
3. unparalleled   7. observation   10. infinite
4. tolerate

Check the one word or phrase that describes what a person is least
likely to do to an opponent.

1. be discourteous to   4. disagree with
2. adore   5. humiliate
3. have malice for

Check the word that has nothing to do with death.

1. assassin   4. secede
2. mourning   5. casket
3. funeral

WORDS WITH MULTIPLE MEANINGS

Circle the letter preceding the word or phrase that is closest to the meaning of the italicized word or phrase from the selection. Numbers in parentheses refer to paragraphs in the selection.

1. His ability finally made a *name for him*. (2)
   a. named him
   b. made him well known
   c. caused him to be given a name
2. What is now the United States might *well* have been divided into several countries. (3)
   a. successfully
   b. easily
   c. quite possibly
3. Several countries with *peculiar* regional interests (3)
   a. unusual
   b. odd
   c. different from those of other regions
4. Keeping the states together as one country has produced *long-range* benefits. (3)
   a. distant
   b. long-lasting
   c. benefits which become apparent in considering the future
5. When the war was *over* (5)
   a. finished
   b. being fought
   c. concerned with

IV. Comprehension of Grammatical Structure

Without looking at the selection, supply the missing words in the following paragraph from the selection.

Lincoln is also admired because _____ his leadership during the difficult _____ of the Civil War. He _____ to do what he thought _____ right at a time when _____ beliefs were unpopular with many _____. He, in a sense, represents _____ spirit of union among the states. Before _____ Civil War, the economy of _____ South depended upon the plantation _____ which made use of slave _____. Reformers in the northern states _____ so much pressure on the southerners _____ free their slaves that some _____ the southern states wanted to _____ from the United States. They _____ that the question of slavery _____ a matter for the individual states to _____ rather than the federal government, _____ they did not want to _____ to its decision. The national _____ in Washington said that no _____ had the right to secede,

_____ the Civil War was the result. _____ the South had won the war, _____ is now the United States _____ well have been divided into _____ countries with peculiar regional interests and problems.

V. Comprehension of Main Ideas and Organizational Pattern

EXERCISE A

This essay is organized by topics. It has a central idea or thesis stated in the first paragraph. The first paragraph also tells what the organization is to be. The essay then develops four points which show why the thesis is true. The last paragraph is a summary. This type of organization is often found in presenting factual material.

Answer the following questions about the essay.

1. What sentence best expresses the central idea?
2. What sentence supports the thesis by showing what the organization is to be?
3. Write the sentence that states the first main supporting idea, or the first reason in support of the thesis.
4. Give three facts in the second paragraph which show that Lincoln fits the popular American ideal of the self-made man.
5. Write the sentence that best expresses the second supporting idea, or the second reason in support of the thesis.
6. For what achievement during the Civil War has Lincoln been greatly praised?
7. Write the sentence that best expresses the third supporting idea.
8. Name three personal qualities of Lincoln that made him popular with his countrymen.
9. Write the sentence that best expresses the fourth supporting idea.
10. Why would the manner in which Lincoln died make him a greater hero?

EXERCISE B

Put the thesis sentence and the sentences containing the four main supporting ideas into the form of an outline. Notice the phrases "first of all," "also," and "furthermore." These are transitional, or connecting, phrases which indicate the beginning of a new supporting idea. Looking for phrases of this sort helps you to follow an author's organization. Your outline will follow the following form:

Thesis sentence:
    I.
    II.
    III.
    IV.

VI. Composition

EXERCISE A

Write a short paragraph answering each of the following questions. Use as many of the new words introduced in this essay as possible.
1. According to the selection you have just read, what are some of the qualities Americans admire most in a hero?
2. What facts of Lincoln's life and personality show that he had some of these qualities?

EXERCISE B

Write a paragraph developing one of the following ideas.
1. _____ is the contemporary American who is best known in my country because. . . .
2. Qualities which make a man great do not always make him easy to live (or work) with.

EXERCISE C

Write a composition of three or four paragraphs on one of the following topics. Organize your composition by dividing your main ideas into subtopics, as is done in the essay on Abraham Lincoln. For example, if you write on "Qualities I admire most in a man," each paragraph can develop or describe one of the qualities. If you write on "The man in my country who is most like Lincoln," each paragraph can give a reason why he is like Lincoln.
1. Qualities I admire most in a man
2. The man in my country who is most like Lincoln
3. Some significant differences between great men and average men

Essay 11

THE ROLE OF WOMEN IN AMERICAN LIFE

Word Study

1. professor /prəfésər/
2. retailer /rítelər/
3. anthropologist /ænθrəpálədʒəst/
4. menial /míníəl/
5. penal /pínəl/
6. managerial /mænədʒíríəl/
7. distinction /dɪstíŋʃən/
8. considerate /kənsídərət/
9. discriminate /dɪskrímənet/

10. aggressive /əgrésɪv/
11. directive /dərékʊv/
12. dignity /dígnətɪ/
13. role /rol/
14. suffrage /sə́frɪdʒ/
15. propaganda /prɑpəgǽndə/
16. orchestra /ɔ́rkəstrə/
17. discipline /dísəplən/

Words with common prefixes or suffixes:

-er, -eur, -or, -ist   noun endings that indicate the person or thing that performs the act
1. *professor*   a teacher, almost always in a college or university
2. *retailer*   a person who retails, or sells something
3. *anthropologist*   one who works in the field of anthropology, a science that studies man, his development, and his culture

-al or *-ial*   adjective endings (related words are given in parentheses)
4. *menial*   pertaining to domestic servants (mean, less important)
5. *penal*   pertaining to punishment for offenses (penalty)
6. *managerial*   referring to management or direction

-tion   noun ending
7. *distinction*   a special recognition; something that separates one thing from other similar ones
-ate   suffix sometimes indicating an adjective and sometimes a verb
8. *considerate* (adjective)   considering, or thinking about, the other person
9. *discriminate* (verb)   to notice the difference between things

Other words that may need definition:
10. *aggressive*   Describing one who is active. An aggressive mother starts many projects and tries to get her family to do the same.

91

11. *directive* having a tendency to tell others what to do and how to do it
12. *dignity* a feeling of self-respect or importance
13. *role* the part one plays in a drama, or the function or office he serves
14. *suffrage* the right to vote
15. *propaganda* a systematic, planned spreading of ideas and practices
16. *orchestra* a group of musicians who perform together on various instruments, mainly stringed instruments
17. *discipline* to train in self-control or obedience

Reading Suggestions
The purpose of this essay is to explain what the role of women in American life is. In explaining this role, the authors also express an attitude toward it. Look for the place where this attitude is stated. Look for the words at the beginning of each paragraph that relate it to the preceding paragraph.

THE ROLE OF WOMEN IN AMERICAN LIFE

1. The position of women in American society is sometimes misunderstood by those from other countries. An example may illustrate. The wife of an American exchange *professor* (1) in Europe, deprived of her electric washer and dryer with which many American homes are equipped, bundled up her washing every week to send to the local laundry. The bundle was rather large, and the family had no car. Therefore it was logical, from the American point of view, for the husband to put the bundle on his bicycle and pedal off to the laundry with it every Monday morning before going to his classes at the university. The professor's wife soon discovered that the neighbors' tongues were busy. One woman whom she knew better than the rest finally approached her.

2. "You shouldn't do that, you know," she said. "It gives people the wrong idea."

3. "I don't understand," said the professor's wife. "I think it is very kind of my husband to take the laundry for me. It is a heavy bundle, and I have a lot of housework to do. In America it is not beneath the *dignity* (12) of a professional man to help his wife."

4. "Oh, it is not your husband that people are talking about," said the neighbor. "They are talking about *you*. Your husband works hard all day; people say you are not *considerate* (8) of him. When he is going to a hard day of work, he shouldn't have to carry the washing first. That's your job."

5. This incident shows that what people believe the duties of men and women to be differs from one country to another. The *role* (13) of women in American culture is difficult to understand unless one has grown up in American society. Women play an important part in American life outside the home at the same time that they are the homemakers. They compete with men in every field of employment. Today one-third of all jobs in the United States are held by women, and their work ranges all the way from *menial* (4) tasks to the professions. The following chart shows the distribution of women in various occupations, as given in the 1968 census.

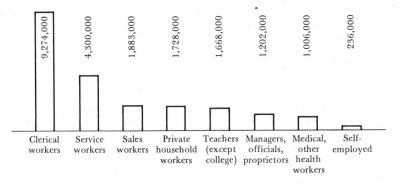

9,274,000	4,300,000	1,883,000	1,728,000	1,668,000	1,202,000	1,006,000	236,000
Clerical workers	Service workers	Sales workers	Private household workers	Teachers (except college)	Managers, officials, proprietors	Medical, other health workers	Self-employed

6. Women predominate in many areas of education. In the elementary schools (through the eighth grade), 85 percent of the teachers are women, as are 46 percent of the teachers in the high schools, although the proportion of men in both types of schools is increasing. In the universities men professors far outnumber women, but women hold professorships in all areas of study, especially literature, music, art, education, social work, and nursing. Women professors are probably more common in American universities than in those of many other countries.

7. Perhaps even more interesting than the number of women employed in American business and industry is the fact that they own 70 to 80 percent of all national wealth such as stocks, bonds, real estate, and savings accounts. These figures are accounted for in part by the fact that women outlive men. Title to a couple's life savings is usually given to the widow upon the death of her husband.

8. In the field of politics women play an important part also. Not many women have been elected to the national Congress, and though there have been women governors of three states, there has never been a woman president. Yet women are so important as voters that no candidate for office can afford not to be aware of their attitudes. Women did not have the right to vote until 1920, but woman *suffrage* (14) did not, as many men predicted, merely double the total number

of votes cast on each side of a question, with the women voting the same as their husbands. Instead, women began to study the issues and candidates and make up their own minds. Today one of the most powerful political organizations is the League of Women Voters. Small local groups meet to study national and international issues, debate the virtues of one course of action as opposed to another, and discuss the qualifications of candidates.

9. Women in the United States have been great reformers. In almost every national reform movement they have played an important part. They spoke and wrote in the cause of freeing the slaves before the Civil War. Harriet Beecher Stowe's novel, *Uncle Tom's Cabin*, was perhaps the most famous single piece of antislavery *propaganda* (15). Women were the first to protest education, property, and divorce laws that *discriminated* (9) against them, and they did not quit protesting until the laws were changed. Dorothea Dix was one of the first American citizens to see the need for reform in mental and *penal* (5) institutions, and many reforms were directly or indirectly made because of her concern. Largely through their own efforts, women were finally given the right to vote by the Nineteenth Amendment to the Constitution.

10. Since that time women have gained other rights that they had not previously had. Increasingly they have been joint owners of property with their husbands or have been able to transact business by themselves. They have become managers of businesses and attained leading positions in the professions. Recently, Woman's Liberation groups, especially the vocal group known as NOW (National Organization of Women) have militantly campaigned for the removal of any differences in pay and job opportunities between men and women, a campaign which resulted in the spring of 1972 in the proposal of an amendment to the Constitution. Reactions to the tactics and demands of these groups have been varied among both men and women, with many giving them strong support and others feeling that women's role in society should still largely be the traditional one of wife and mother, and that her job outside the home should be secondary. Yet larger and larger numbers of women are working outside the home, many of them fulfilling dual roles of career woman and homemaker.

11. Regardless of woman's rights, in the United States a woman is much more nearly a partner in the household than she is in many other parts of the world. Family decisions in the matters of finance, religion, politics, policies of training the children, health, and recreation are generally the result of discussion between husband and wife. The women may or may not help the husband in his business. Wives of farmers, of small business men, and of ministers are most likely to do this.

12. If the woman does not work outside the home, she is largely responsible for the housekeeping. If she does work, the husband and wife may share the responsibilities, the husband helping with the housework more than may be usual in some other countries, particularly in countries where it is easier to hire household servants. In household duties, much of the responsibility for disciplining the children and of supervising their schoolwork falls upon the mother. The father may help the children with their homework, but the mother generally sees to it that they get the homework done. She is the one who usually has conferences with her children's teachers about their progress in school and who most often represents the family at parent-teacher association meetings.

13. Women do 80 to 85 percent of America's household shopping. The advertising in department stores and small shops is largely directed toward the woman buyer. Radio, television, and magazines all reflect the eagerness of both manufacturers and *retailers* (2) to capture the interest of women in their product. A firm may spend as much as $2,750,000 per issue for advertising space in a leading woman's magazine.

14. Margaret Mead, an *anthropologist* (3), speaks of the "*aggressive* (10), *directive* (11) American mothers." The tasks that fall upon her to do make the American mother aggressive and directive. If she were not, she would not finish all that is expected of her. (*1279 words*)

EXERCISES

I. Comprehension of Details
Choose the sentence fragment that best completes each of the following. The exact statement may not appear directly in the essay.

1. In America, if a husband helps his wife with the housework,
   a. the neighbors criticize her.
   b. the neighbors criticize him.
   c. the neighbors think he is considerate.
   d. the neighbors think that the wife does not work.
2. This situation exists because
   a. women are glorified in America.
   b. men in America are easily bossed by women.
   c. women in America have heavy household duties and little household help.
   d. American men are not dignified.
3. In the employment world in the United States
   a. women have equal positions with men in every case and are given equal preference when hiring is done.

     b. there are more women clerks than women teachers.

     c. women expect and receive many concessions from men.

     d. women dominate in many fields, especially heavy labor.

4. In the field of politics, since they were given the right to vote in the United States in 1920,

     a. women have usually voted in the same way as their husbands, and thus their vote counts for little.

     b. women have made equal achievements with men both in voting and office-holding.

     c. women have far surpassed men in working for good government through the League of Women Voters.

     d. women have shown interest in good government through study of issues and qualifications of candidates.

5. American women who work outside the home

     a. usually have little interest in the home.

     b. leave the major responsibility for the home to their husbands.

     c. in the majority of cases generally consider themselves primarily as homemakers.

     d. usually have servants to do their housework for them.

6. In family decisions about household purchasing

     a. women generally make the final decisions about major household items and do the purchasing.

     b. the man controls how the money is to be spent, and, as a rule, the wife has nothing to say about it.

     c. the husband and wife usually talk over the advisability of buying major equipment, though the woman may do the actual purchasing.

     d. the man usually does the actual purchasing.

7. Women own

     a. 20 to 30% of all the national wealth in the U.S.A.

     b. 40 to 50% of all the national wealth in the U.S.A.

     c. 70 to 80% of all the national wealth in the U.S.A.

8. American women like to feel

     a. that their intelligence amazes the men, so that the men will defer to them.

     b. that they can work outside their home if they want to.

     c. that they dominate the men in the professional world.

     d. that they dominate the men in the home.

9. Figures show that in the United States

     a. women are mostly employed for menial positions.

     b. women are mostly employed for positions that hold some dignity.

     c. more women than men teach in grade schools.

     d. while there are many women factory workers and clerks, there are practically no women in executive positions.

10. In spite of the important role played by women in American
    society,
    a. one is still not justified in believing that society is run by
       women.
    b. one is correct in assuming that American society revolves
       about women.
    c. men are relatively unimportant in American business and
       economic life.
    d. one is justified in believing that women are more important
       than men.

II. Skimming Exercise

Since this selection gives more details, facts, and figures than the
preceding one, it cannot be skimmed so quickly for general mastery
of content. You can, however, skim to locate the topics being discussed. Then you may want to read carefully the paragraph dealing
with the topic to pick up details about it.

EXERCISE A

Find the number of the paragraph that discusses each of the following.
1. woman's role in politics
2. woman's role in making family decisions
3. women as reformers
4. women in education
5. women's responsibility in disciplining the children
6. women in business and industry
7. women's role in family shopping

EXERCISE B

What two groups might the above topics be separated into? Which
items go in each group?

III. Vocabulary Exercises

WORD STUDY

Indicate whether each of the following statements is true or false
by writing the letter T or F in the space provided.
_____ 1. A *professor* might be an *anthropologist.*
_____ 2. A *professor* holds a *menial* position in America.
_____ 3. A *considerate* person would probably not be put in a *penal*
           institution.
_____ 4. A *retailer* might sell *refrigerators.*
_____ 5. A *managerial* position requires a certain amount of *dignity.*
_____ 6. A person in a *managerial* position does not have to be
           aggressive or *directive* in any way.

_____ 7. Women have *suffrage* in the United States.
_____ 8. An *orchestra* is a *plumber's* union.
_____ 9. A *plumber* lays *linoleum* for a living.
_____10. One who cannot tell red from green is not able to *discriminate* between colors.

IDIOMATIC AND 'FIGURATIVE LANGUAGE
Circle the letter preceding the sentence in which the italicized word has a meaning most like that of the essay. Numbers in parentheses refer to paragraphs in the essay.
1. Women began to study the issues and candidates and *make up* their own minds. (8)
   a. I hope you will *make up* for lost time.
   b. The people who *make up* this group come from many different countries.
   c. You will have to *make up* a report on this.
2. The most famous *single* piece of antislavery propaganda. . . . (9)
   a. We didn't go swimming a *single* time last summer.
   b. We played *singles* in the tennis match.
   c. This is a *single* room, not a double one.
3. She is the one who *sees to* it that they get their homework done. (12)
   a. I will *see to* your request in a minute.
   b. I will *see* you *to* your room.
   c. On a clear day you can *see to* the mountains.
4. The tasks that *fall upon* her to do make the American mother aggressive and directive.
   a. The hungry dog *fell upon* his dinner.
   b. The blame for the accident *fell upon* the driver of the car.
   c. The tree *fell upon* the roof.

IV. Comprehension of Grammatical Structure
In the following paragraphs supply the correct form of the indicated verb in each of the blanks.

The wife an American exchange professor in Europe, _____ (deprive) of her electric washer and dryer with which many American homes _____ (equip), bundled up her washing every week _____ (send) it to the local laundry. The bundle was rather large, and the family had no car. Therefore it was logical, from the American point of view, for the husband _____ (put) the bundle on his bicycle and pedal off to the laundry with it every Monday morning before _____ (go) to his classes at the university.

One of her neighbors said to her, "You shouldn't _____ (do) that, you know."

"I don't understand," said the professor's wife. "I think it is very kind of my husband _____ (take) the laundry for me. It is a heavy bundle, and I have a lot of housework _____ (do). In America it is not beneath the dignity of a professional man _____ (help) his wife."

"Oh, it is not your husband that people _____ (talk) about," said the neighbor. "They _____ (talk) about *you*. People say you are not considerate of your husband. When he _____ (go) to a hard day of work, he shouldn't have _____ (carry) the washing first. That's your job."

This incident shows that what people believe the duties of men and women _____ (be) _____ (differ) from one country to another.

V. Comprehension of Main Ideas and Organizational Pattern

1. The first five paragraphs of this essay are introductory. What is the purpose of the illustration in paragraphs 1–4?
2. Paragraph 5 contains a sentence that best states the thesis or central idea of the essay. What sentence is this?
3. What aspect of the role of women in American society is the subject of paragraphs 5–9?
4. What new aspect of the role of American women is introduced in paragraph 10?
5. What paragraphs deal with this topic?
6. What sentence in paragraph 5 indicates that two aspects of the role of American women will be discussed?
7. How many paragraphs of the essay are conclusion?
8. To develop an idea or explain an attitude or belief, an author uses various types of supporting material. Some of the more common are: (1) facts and figures, (2) statistics, (3) examples, (4) illustrative anecdotes, (5) descriptions, (6) explanations of principles or of how things operate, (7) quotation from an authority, (8) comparison and contrast. Paragraph 8 uses facts and figures. Find an example of another paragraph developed in this same way.
9. Paragraph 9 uses examples. Find another paragraph developed in this same way.

VI. Composition

EXERCISE A
Write a paragraph discussing the following.
Name three fields of endeavor in business or community life in America where women have played important roles, and give a specific example of something they have done in each field.

EXERCISE B
What kind of supporting material discussed in exercise V (facts and figures, statistics, illustrations, explanations, etc.) would you use to

develop a paragraph beginning with and developing one of the following topic sentences?

1. Recently I witnessed an incident that impressed me with the difference between the status of women in the United States and in my own country.
2. There are several reasons why I think it is better for a wife to stay at home and not try to hold a job.
3. I find certain faults (advantages) in the American attitude toward women.

EXERCISE C

What plan of organization would you use in writing an essay of three or four paragraphs on one of the following topics? What would your main divisions be? Make an outline for an essay on the topic. Indicate the purpose and the main supporting points. Then write the essay.

1. Qualities that I would like my wife (husband) to have
2. The role of women in my country
3. Division of responsibilities between my mother and father
4. Why I would (would not) marry an American man (woman)

Essay 12

THE AMERICAN EDUCATIONAL SYSTEM: ORGANIZATION

Word Study

1. kindergarten /kíndərgɑrtən/
2. parochial /pərókiəl/
3. coeducational /koɛdʒəkéʃənəl/
4. consolidated /kənsɑ́lədetəd/
5. elementary /ɛləméntəri/
6. secondary /sékəndɛri/
7. academic /ækədémɪk/
8. vocational /vokéʃənəl/
9. compulsory /kəmpə́lsəri/
10. certificate /sərtífɪkət/
11. diploma /dɪplómə/
12. graduation /grædʒuéʃən/
13. accrediting /əkrédɪtɪŋ/
14. integrate /íntəgret/
15. specialize /spéʃəlaɪz/
16. curriculum /kəríkyələm/
17. tuition /tuíʃən/
18. illiterate /ɪlítərət/
19. scholastic /skəlǽstɪk/
20. electorate /əléktərət/
21. automatic /ɔtəmǽtɪk/
22. rigid /rídʒɪd/
23. adequately /ǽdəkwətli/
24. assessed /əsést/

Words used to indicate kinds of schools:
1. *kindergarten* a school attended by children, about 5 years old, before they begin the first grade
2. *parochial* An adjective related to the noun *parish*. A *parochial* school is one supported and controlled by a church.
3. *coeducational* A *coeducational* school is one in which both boys and girls are taught. *Co-* is a prefix meaning "together."
4. *consolidated* combined (A *consolidated* school is made up of several different schools of the same kind that have been put together.)
5. *elementary* *Elementary* schools are ones that prepare a student for more advanced study. They teach him the *elements*, or basic principles, and generally consist of grades one through six.
6. *secondary* *Secondary* schools are the high schools, which come after preparatory (elementary) education. They correspond to the European gymnasium.

Adjectives used to indicate kinds of education:
7. *academic* An adjective from the noun *academy*, historically a school that prepared students for the university. An academy is also a body of learned men. An *academic* education is a literary or classical, rather than technical, education.
8. *vocational* *Vocational* education prepares one for a vocation, a trade or occupation.
9. *compulsory* required (*Compulsory* education is education that is required by law.)

Nouns used in talking about completing school work:
10. *certificate* a paper stating that a student has completed the study of certain courses or has made certain achievement
11. *diploma* a certificate received at the end of a course of study, such as one would get in a high school or university
12. *graduation* a ceremony at which one receives a diploma

Words often used when discussing school problems:
13. *accrediting* giving a statement that an institution has met set standards
14. *integrate* to make something part of a whole (A foreign-born person is *integrated* into a new culture when he becomes a part of it.)
15. *specialize* In the field of education, "to specialize" means to study a special or particular field or subject, rather than to study things in general.
16. *curriculum* a course of study or a program of studies (plural: *curricula*) (The subjects that a school offers make up its *curriculum*.)
17. *tuition* a sum of money that is paid for instruction
18. *illiterate* one who is unable to read or write (This word is used both as a noun and as an adjective: He is an *illiterate*. He is *illiterate*.)
19. *scholastic* an adjective related to the noun *scholar*, a person who studies

Other new words in this selection:
20. *electorate* the body of people entitled to vote in an election
21. *automatic* done by itself, or without conscious thought
22. *rigid* stiff (A *rigid* law is one that is never changed.)
23. *adequately* satisfactorily, suitably
24. *assessed* have a value set on (present tense — *assess*)

Reading Suggestions
The organizational pattern of this essay is not so obvious as that of many of the essays you have read in this book. Its purpose — to tell how the American school system operates — is indicated only in-

directly. The introduction (the first paragraph) explains the philosophy of American education that accounts for its organization and curriculum. Look for the statement of this philosophy. Each of paragraphs 2–12 deals with one aspect of American education. In order to see how the details of the essay fit together, look for the topic of each paragraph.

THE AMERICAN EDUCATIONAL SYSTEM: ORGANIZATION

1. The American educational system, like that of any other country, has grown up to meet the needs of the particular environment in which it developed, and it reflects the history of the country. Thus it differs somewhat from the systems of other countries. Perhaps its most distinctive feature is its emphasis on education of the masses rather than on education of the intellectuals. The philosophy of the American educational system is that a democracy depends upon a fully informed *electorate* (20), and that therefore each citizen should receive the best education that it is possible for him to receive. As a result, in America most children in the same community attend school together from *kindergarten* (1) through high school regardless of differences in intellectual ability or in family background. There are a small number of private *secondary* (6) schools and an even smaller number of private *elementary* (5) schools where a fee is charged and children are accepted or rejected on the basis of an examination. But the great majority of American children attend the free, state-supported public schools which are open to everyone without an entrance examination, even at the secondary level.

2. Since separation of church and state is a principle of American democracy and, therefore, religion cannot be taught in state-supported schools, there are also many *parochial* (2), or church-supported, schools, usually Catholic. These schools do not receive tax money, and a fee is often paid by the parents of each child attending. The parochial schools must meet requirements set up by state and other *accrediting* (13) agencies, and therefore the program of study, with the exception of the religious emphasis, is much like that of the tax-supported schools. Most public schools are *coeducational* (3), but many of the parochial schools, especially at the secondary level, are for boys or girls only.

3. Educational policies and *curricula* (16) are set up by the individual state organizations established for the purpose rather than by the federal government, but the general plan varies only slightly from state to state. There are eight years of elementary schooling, not including the kindergarten, which is a part of the public school system in many places, especially the cities. The elementary school

is followed by four years of secondary school, or high school. Often the last two years of elementary and the first years of secondary school are combined into a junior high school.

4. The school year is nine months in length, beginning early in September and continuing until about the first of June, with a vacation of a week or two at Christmas time and sometimes a shorter one in the spring. There are slight variations from place to place. Students enter the first grade at the age of six, and attendance is *compulsory* (9) in most states until the age of sixteen or until the student has finished the eighth grade. Here again, the practice varies slightly from state to state, but each state has a compulsory school attendance law. Though the percentage varies from region to region, the proportion of *illiterates* (18) throughout the United States as a whole is less than one percent, and it is the boast of the American people that free elementary schools are within the reach of everyone and free high schools are in all but the most isolated regions.

5. The elementary schools tend to be small, generally serving families within the immediate area, although agitation for equal educational opportunity for people of all races and economic levels has resulted in some areas in busing students across town. The high schools are generally larger and accommodate pupils from four or five elementary schools. A small town generally has several elementary schools and one high school. Particularly in larger communities, the problems created by busing children of both elementary and high school age for long distances from their homes in order to obtain racial and economic balance in the schools became a national issue in 1972, as many parents objected to taking children out of their home communities and to the length of time spent in travel. Since schools have been largely supported by local taxes, schools in affluent areas have been able to provide better educational facilities and attract better teachers by better pay. Means other than busing are being sought to provide equal schooling for all.

6. Perhaps the greatest difference between the American and foreign school systems is at the high school level. Admission to the American high school is *automatic* (21) on completion of the elementary school, and one high school attempts to meet the needs of all students. The American high school offers the types of courses that are usually found in separate schools in Europe. With increasingly large high schools, a wide variety of courses is possible. Thus in the same school one student could *specialize* (15) in home economics, another in chemistry and physics, another in Latin and the humanities, and yet another in automobile mechanics. Differences in ability and in *vocational* (8) or professional goals are taken care of as far as possible by variation in curriculum.

7. During the four-year high school program, the student studies

four or five major subjects per year, and classes in each of these subjects meet for an hour a day, five days a week. In addition, the student usually has classes in physical education, music, and art several times a week. If he fails a course, he repeats only that course and not the work of the entire year. Students must complete a certain number of courses in order to receive a *diploma* (11), or *certificate* (10) of *graduation* (12).

8. Public education extends beyond high school. About 56 percent of the high school graduates in the United States spend some time pursuing further *academic* (7) education in colleges or universities. This does not include those who attend trade schools of various types. Nearly every state has at least one university supported by public funds which offers training through the Doctor of Philosophy degree. In addition, there are often public community junior colleges, which offer a two-year program in the liberal arts or in practical subjects. State teachers colleges, which specialized in training both elementary and secondary schoolteachers, have now generally expanded their offerings to include other fields and have become state universities. The main difference between a college and a university is that the latter is a collection of colleges, each of which specializes in a different field. Thus, a university will have a college of engineering, a college of liberal arts, a college of education (teachers college), a college of law, a college of medicine, and so on.

9. Free public education was the original American ideal but increasingly students at all levels pay many different kinds of fees. The state colleges and universities charge a small fee for *tuition* (17) or registration. This fee is higher for those who come from outside the state. Many scholarships are available, however, and the schools help students to find employment. Working one's way through college is commonplace, and schools often adjust the student's program of studies so that he can work part of the time. Even in elementary and secondary schools where no tuition is charged, there are sometimes fees for textbooks and student activities.

10. Usually there is no admission examination required by a state university for those who have finished high school within the state. Sometimes a certain pattern of high school studies is necessary, however, and most state universities require a certain *scholastic* (19) average, or average of high school grades. This liberal admission policy results from the theory that if the state university is supported largely by state funds, any resident of the state should have the opportunity to attend. A student with a poor scholastic record in high school may fail all his courses and have to leave school at the end of the first semester, but at least he has had the opportunity.

11. Not all of the 56 percent of high school graduates who go on to college go to state-supported schools, however. Private colleges and

universities, especially the larger, well-known ones such as Harvard, Princeton, and Yale, have had *rigid* (22) scholastic requirements for entrance, including an examination. In the late 1960s and early 1970s, with passage of Civil Rights legislation by the federal and state governments, there has been a move to open universities to people who, because of economic conditions, may have poor educational backgrounds and could not meet the ordinary entrance requirements. While there have been some outstanding cases of students who have been successful, others have been disappointing and the effect of this plan on the educational system cannot yet be assessed (24).

12. Because of the nature of the American high school and the admission policies of colleges and universities, the first two years in an American college or university differ somewhat from a similar period in a European one. These years in an American college, especially in a large state university with a liberal admission policy, are looked on as a trial period during which a certain scholastic record must be maintained if a student is to be allowed to complete his bachelor's degree. In a sense, these two years are a continuation of secondary education. During this time certain courses in English, social science, natural science, and so forth must usually be completed before a student may begin an intensive study of his special field. It usually takes four years to meet the requirements for a Bachelor of Arts or Bachelor of Science (B.A.) degree. A Master of Arts or Master of Science degree (M.A.) may be obtained in one or two additional years. The highest academic degree is the Doctor of Philosophy (Ph.D.). It may take any number of years to complete the original research work necessary to obtain this degree.

13. In the American system of education there are certain difficulties that arise from trying to educate everyone together. The "American dream" for meeting the educational needs of everyone has not always been fulfilled. This and other problems will be discussed in the next essay. Many Americans feel, however, that the system has many advantages. Although the ideal sometimes exceeds the reality, an attempt is made to provide equal opportunity for all. Above all, the American educational system has been a factor in breaking down class barriers, in *integrating* (14) children of various ethnic backgrounds into the pattern of American life, and in giving the country a sense of unity. (*1724 words*)

EXERCISES

I. Comprehension of Details

Choose the sentence fragment that best completes each of the following.

1. American education is based on the philosophy of
   a. placing particular stress on education of the intellectuals.
   b. educating each citizen as fully as possible.
   c. neglecting the intellectuals in favor of the masses.
   d. training a class of leaders.
2. In the United States church schools
   a. receive state funds.
   b. differ radically in educational policy from public schools.
   c. exist only in very small numbers.
   d. do not receive tax money because of the policy of separation of church and state.
3. Educational policies in the various states
   a. show little uniformity.
   b. are uniform because education is controlled by the federal government.
   c. vary somewhat because they are under local control.
   d. vary somewhat in spite of federal control.
4. The high schools in the United States
   a. tend to be small because they serve only a small local community.
   b. tend to be small because they emphasize one course of study only.
   c. tend to be large because they offer a wide variety of courses.
   d. tend to be large because Americans like to display big buildings.
5. In an American high school
   a. a student usually studies four or five major subjects per year.
   b. because of the wide selection of courses, a student usually takes a large number of different ones at the same time.
   c. each class meets for one hour a week.
   d. if a student fails one subject, he must repeat the work of the entire year.
6. The state-supported universities in the United States
   a. are open only to graduates of certain academic high schools.
   b. have very rigid entrance requirements.
   c. operate on the theory that any resident of the state should have the opportunity to attend.
   d. admit only graduates of public high schools.

7. In order to attend a state-supported university,
   a. it is not necessary to pay tuition.
   b. one must pay a high fee.
   c. residents of the state need not pay a fee, but nonresidents must.
   d. even residents of the state must pay a fee of some sort.
8. The first two years in an American university
   a. are to a certain extent a continuation of secondary education.
   b. entitle a student to the Bachelor of Arts or Bachelor of Science degree.
   c. are a period of intense specialization in the field of major interest of the student.
   d. are much more difficult than the following years.
9. Of all those who graduate from an American high school
   a. about 56 percent receive the Doctor of Philosophy degree.
   b. about 56 percent receive the Master of Arts or Master of Science degree.
   c. about 56 percent receive the Bachelor of Arts or Bachelor of Science degree.
   d. about 56 percent spend some time in an institution of higher education.
10. One advantage of the American school system is that
    a. its ideals are always carried out in reality.
    b. it has been an integrating factor in American culture.
    c. it divides society along class lines.
    d. it instructs the average person but not the intellectual.

II. Skimming Exercise

As quickly as possible, find the number of the paragraph which has each of the following as its main topic.
1. The length of time an American child generally spends in elementary and secondary school
2. The size and location of elementary and secondary schools
3. The numbers and kinds of schools offering public education beyond the university level
4. The number of courses a high school student usually takes and how often these courses meet
5. The types of courses offered in a typical high school in the United States
6. The characteristics of the first two years of an American college or university
7. Admission policies in American colleges and universities
8. Financial support of American colleges and universities

III. Vocabulary Exercises

WORD STUDY

From each of the following groups pick the word or phrase that is closest in meaning to the italicized word.

1. *scholastic*   academic, diploma preparatory, coeducational
2. *vocational*   scholastic, occupational, special, loud
3. *consolidate*   graduate, build, combine, admit
4. *illiterate*   unintelligent, intelligent, erase, uneducated
5. *diploma*   statesman, certificate, parish, greeting
6. *integrate*   adequate, become part of, require, rigid
7. *electorate*   consolidate, group of school officials, group of people who vote, group of people who live in the same parish
8. *compulsory*   required, traditional, built, combined
9. *rigid*   changing, stiff, required, easy
10. *parochial*   required, scholastic, course of study, belonging to a parish

WORDS WITH MULTIPLE MEANINGS

Circle the letter preceding the sentence which best illustrates the meaning of the italicized word in each of the following. Numbers in parentheses refer to paragraphs in the essay.

1. *Since* separation of church and state is a principle of American democracy . . . there are many parochial, or church-supported, schools. (2)
   a. I have not seen you *since* last week.
   b. *Since* you are here, you can help us.
   c. *Since* you have been here, it has rained every day.
2. The parochial schools must meet requirements *set up* by state and other accrediting agencies. (2)
   a. He *set up* the equipment for the game.
   b. He *set up* the ladder against the wall.
   c. We *set up* the program for the evening.
3. and *yet* another in automobile mechanics (6)
   a. I am not ready to go *yet*.
   b. We would like to sign the agreement; *yet* it does not seem advisable.
   c. There is more *yet* to come.
4. High school graduates spend *some* time pursuing further academic education (8)
   a. We hope to go *sometime*.
   b. They had to walk *some* distance in order to get there.
   c. We spent *some* money at the store.

5. Sometimes a *certain* pattern of high school studies is necessary. (10)
   a. I was not *certain* that I could come.
   b. There is a *certain* principle that seems to be operating here.
   c. Do you have to be there at any *certain* time?
6. It usually *takes* four years to meet the requirements. (12)
   a. How long will it *take* you to get here?
   b. Will you *take* me with you?
   c. I would like to *take* a trip.

IV. Comprehension of Grammatical Structure

If the word *that* in each of the sentences below is a pronoun, write the word or word group it stands for or is substituted for. If it is not a pronoun, write *no* in the space provided. Numbers in parentheses refer to the paragraph of the essay in which the sentence occurs.

1. The American educational system, like *that* of any other country, has grown up to meet the needs of the particular environment in which it developed. (1) _____
2. The philosophy of the American educational system is *that* a democracy depends upon a fully informed electorate. (1) _____
3. Each citizen should receive the best education *that* it is possible for him to receive. (1) _____
4. The program of study is much like *that* of the tax-supported schools. (2) _____
5. It is the boast of the American people *that* free elementary schools are within the reach of everyone. (4) _____
6. The American high school offers the types of courses *that* are usually found in separate schools in Europe. (6) _____
7. If he fails a course, he repeats only *that* course. (7) _____
8. The main difference between a college and a university is *that* the latter is a collection of colleges. (8) _____

V. Comprehension of Main Ideas and Organizational Pattern

Taking brief notes can help you remember the content of what you read. These notes should indicate in brief form the important points about the main topic of each paragraph.

Note the central idea of paragraph 1 of the essay. Your notes might read something like the following:

Basic philosophy of American education:
   Emphasis on education of the masses to ensure enlightened people to carry on democracy.
Result:
   Children in a community generally attend school together regardless of differences in ability or background. Most attend free state-supported schools.

Following this pattern, take brief notes on the entire essay.

VI. Composition

EXERCISE A

Write a paragraph answering one of the following questions about the American educational system. You may refer to the notes you took in Exercise V.

1. What are the various types of schools in the United States according to method of support, and what are the admission requirements?
2. How many years does a student ordinarily spend at each level of education through secondary school in the United States, and how does he progress from one level to another?
3. What are some ways in which state universities in the United States may differ from private liberal arts colleges?

EXERCISE B

In preparation for an essay on the differences between the American educational system and the educational system in your own country, make a list of the areas in which American education differs from education in your country. Your list might include such areas as the following: (1) methods of support, (2) curriculum, (3) length of time in the elementary school, (4) length of time in the secondary school, (5) types of degrees given by universities.

You should limit your subject in some way. You might limit it in scope. For example, you might want to write on the differences in the types of secondary schools found in the two countries, or on the differences in the ways examinations are conducted, or on the differences in the two university systems. Or you might limit it by taking a point of view, by showing, for example, that the differences are not as great as they are generally thought to be, or that the two countries have developed different philosophies because of their historical development.

Formulate your central idea in a single sentence which the essay as a whole will develop. Make some notes on the topic you want to cover, and write the essay. Hand in your notes and the statement of your central idea with your paper, as directed by your instructor. The statement of your central idea should be clearly made in the introductory paragraph of your essay.

THE AMERICAN EDUCATIONAL SYSTEM: PROBLEMS

Word Study

1. circumstance /sɔ́rkəmstæns/
2. attainment /əténmənt)
3. rigorous /rígərəs/
4. acute /əkyút/
5. differentiate /dɪfəréntʃɪet/
6. elite /elít/

7. potentiality /potɛnʃɪǽlətɪ/
8. evaluate /ivǽlyuet/
9. segment /sɛ́gmənt/
10. discrepancy /dɪskrépənsi/
11. expenditure /ekspéndɪtʃər/

The following are definitions of the above words (related words which you may or may not know are given in parentheses).

1. *circumstance* a condition affecting a person (circumstantial)
2. *attainment* act of gaining something through effort (attain, attainable, attainability)
3. *rigorous* strict or severe (rigor)
4. *acute* severe or sharp, as an acute pain or an acute problem (acuteness)
5. *differentiate* to set apart because of a particular quality or difference (differ, difference, different, differentiation)
6. *elite* those most carefully selected, as the Elite Guard
7. *potentiality* character or condition that may be possible (potential, potentially)
8. *evaluate* to place a value on (value, evaluation, valuable)
9. *segment* a section, a part of a whole (segmental, segmentary)
10. *discrepancy* lack of agreement, difference
11. *expenditure* a using up of time or money (expend, expendable, expense, expensive)

Reading Suggestions

The title of this selection indicates that the essay will deal with problems in American education. The introduction consists of a long illustration followed by a paragraph that states the two types of problems which will be discussed. In order to follow the author's organization and thus comprehend his ideas better, look for this paragraph. Then read for an understanding of the two types of problems. Look for words like *solved* or *solution* which point to possible solutions to the problems. Note whether these words are qualified by expressions such as *possible, proposed, attempted,* or *might be, may be,* or *could be.* The last part of the essay compares the success of the American and European school systems. Look for the paragraph where this comparison begins.

THE AMERICAN EDUCATIONAL SYSTEM: PROBLEMS

1. An English mother recently complained that her eight-year-old son must attend the local "board" school, roughly the equivalent of the American public school. The boy's father was a clergyman in a parish in a laboring man's section of a medium-sized city, and the school was therefore attended largely by children of laborers. "He is learning poor English from them," complained his mother. "The school is not suited to the needs of those who will attend a university or even a good secondary school. With what he learns there, our boy will certainly never win a scholarship to a university-preparatory secondary school and probably couldn't pass the entrance examination anyway. We can't afford to send him to another elementary school, so I'm afraid he'll never go to the university. What would a person in similar *circumstances* (1) in the United States do about his son's education?"

2. These particular problems are not the most important ones in American education. For one thing, there is not the difference in types of schools. In similar circumstances in the United States the boy would go to school with the laboring men's children just as he is doing in England, and he might learn some poor English from the other children. However, since in most cases the laboring men are products of the same kind of public elementary and secondary schools as the men in the professions, their children may speak English that is little different from that of the sons of professional men. Instruction and standards of achievement vary from school to school depending upon the academic ability and the interests of the majority of the students and the amount of money the community has available for education. Still, there is a degree of uniformity because state and regional accrediting agencies insist that certain standards be maintained and certain things be taught. Teachers' organizations encourage the use of standardized achievement tests so that a student may compare his *attainment* (2) with that of students from schools not only in other parts of the community but in other states as well.

3. After this boy finished an American elementary school, whether in a laboring man's neighborhood or not, he would be able to go on to the public high school, which would offer college-preparatory training. The examination that most European students must take at the age of twelve or thirteen, which determines future schooling and to a certain degree choice of a profession, does not exist in America. His high school diploma would allow him to enter the state university, unless his academic records were very poor. If his grades in high school were high enough, he could get a scholarship that would pay most of his expenses. In a state university perhaps the proportion of a class doing outstanding work might not be so great as the proportion at Harvard, or at Oxford or Cambridge in England, because the average academic ability of those entering would not be so high. However, the group at the top in a state university would compare favorably with students in schools with more *rigorous* (3) admission policies, and he could receive a good education there.

4. The American educational system is designed to take care of the problems raised by the English mother, and it boasts of giving equal opportunity to all. Yet because of its nature and the philosophy of education it represents, the system gives rise to certain problems of its own. In addition it faces the problems common to any educational system and attempts to meet them in accordance with its own particular philosophy.

5. The greatest problem that arises from the nature of the American educational system comes about as a result of trying to educate everyone together. Although the system does offer many opportunities to the average person—opportunities to develop his particular skills and abilities and to try to get as much academic education as he can absorb—a pressing problem is how to challenge the person of above-average academic ability and at the same time take care of the needs of the person with average ability. The problem exists to a degree in the elementary school, as there is a tendency to adjust teaching to the level of the class, but it becomes *acute* (4) at the high school level where differences in interests, backgrounds, vocational plans, and other factors in addition to academic ability enter in.

6. The problem is solved in part by *differentiated* (5) curricula. There is a wide variety of course offerings in an American high school, and students are allowed to choose a certain number of the subjects they study. Presumably the student who has neither the academic interest nor the ability to do college work will not take courses such as college-preparatory algebra, advanced chemistry, or third-year Latin. In spite of the guidance systems set up to help students make their choices, however, there are always a certain number who pick courses for which they are unsuited. Until they drop or fail the course, they sometimes slow down the progress of

the class. A greater difficulty arises from the fact that in the usual type of comprehensive high school certain courses are required of all students. These usually include two years of English, two years of mathematics, and at least one laboratory science. In such basic courses students are sometimes separated into different classes according to ability or according to their vocational plans. Thus some students will study English and American literature in their English courses while others study business English and letter writing. In small schools, such a separation is not possible, and the tendency to plan the course for the average student is a factor to contend with.

7. At the college level, particularly in state-supported schools with a liberal admission policy, this problem still exists. The general courses offered in the first two years are often designed to round out the education of the average person rather than to appeal merely to the specialist in a field, and there is much debate in educational circles over what the standard of performance for the "average" person at this level should be. "These courses are too easy," say some. "We must uphold standards." "Is it democratic," asks another group, "to set requirements so high and make the courses so difficult that only the intellectually *elite* (6), not the average citizen who forms the backbone of our country, can profit by them?" In more specialized fields in the third and fourth years and especially at the graduate level, the problem is less acute because the attempt is usually to make standards rigorous enough so that students whose special abilities do not lie in that particular field will drop out.

8. Not only is there a problem of standards. Perhaps an even greater problem in recent years, when larger and larger numbers of students are continuing their education in high schools and in colleges and universities beyond the compulsory limit, is the matter of "relevance." Both students and educators are constantly asking what courses are more relevant or useful in their future lives. American society places a great stress on a college education as the pathway to success in business, and a college graduate is more apt to be hired by a business firm than one who has had no college training. Yet many are questioning whether the kind of academic training offered in college, and even in high school, is what the student really needs for jobs such as carpenter, policeman, or office clerk. The fact is that many students are in courses in which they see little value. Some educators are questioning whether a revision of the system might not be in order to offer more vocational and technical training and more types of college degrees, if society is to demand a college education.

9. Educators are keenly aware of the difficulties that lie in the way of educating everyone together. There is the problem of the point to which such education should go. There is the problem of keeping

the poorer students from holding back the better ones or being satisfied with a level beneath their abilities. The solutions that have been tried are sometimes, though not always, successful. There is always the danger that "equal opportunity for all" may be interpreted to mean "the same education for all" regardless of differences in ability and need.

10. For problems that are not merely characteristic of the educational system of the United States but that all systems must face, the attempted solutions also reflect the philosophy upon which American education is based — the philosophy that everyone should be given the opportunity to develop his greatest *potentiality* (7). One of the major problems is the question of what should be the true goal of education. Is it to master facts or to develop the mind and spirit? While different educational systems may agree on the soundness of the latter goal, they may differ on the interpretation of what this means and on the best way to carry it out. The American system tends to interpret it to mean understanding man and society in order to get along with oneself and in the community. Learning to think for oneself and learning by doing are stressed as means of developing the character and judgment that will help one achieve these goals. Thus discussion plays a large part in the classroom, and teachers are urged to encourage self-expression. The American high school youth is usually quite ready to give an opinion on almost any subject. Through courses in composition and public speaking he learns effective methods of presenting his ideas.

11. The emphasis on learning by doing is one of the reasons for the large number of extracurricular activities that characterize the American high school. These activities serve a unique function in the educational pattern. Most of them foster special skills and interests that develop out of classroom activities, but some exist purely to provide recreation.

12. Public speaking activities, school publications, student government organizations, as well as the great variety of school clubs are a few examples of activities of this type. High school extracurricular speech activities attempt to develop skills needed in a democratic society. The high school paper and the annual, or yearbook, give students training in the field of publication beyond what they get in their regular courses in English. The student council, or student government organization, discusses certain school problems and determines policy.

13. The extent to which the American school system lives up to its ideal of providing equal opportunity to develop mind and spirit to the fullest possible extent is, again, a debatable question. Is the school's interpretation of what it means to develop mind and character broad enough? Does it make too great a distinction between

developing the mind and spirit on the one hand and mastering facts on the other? The American system prides itself on offering students more than mere memorization of facts; yet it must guard against going too far in the opposite direction. Self-expression and discussion in the classroom are admirable learning experiences. Yet to explain oneself intelligently one must have knowledge of facts as a basis for discussion. Extracurricular activities have much to recommend them. Yet there is the danger that students will be kept so busy with activities that academic learning is neglected.

14. When we try to *evaluate* (8) how good a job the American public schools do, the American high school graduate is often compared with the graduate of a European gymnasium, or college-preparatory secondary school, and it is contended that the European knows more facts. A European student who has graduated from a gymnasium may, in some respects, be more nearly at the educational level of an American student in his second year of college. Critics of the American system say that this is the result of educating everyone together and of placing too much emphasis on extracurricular activities. There may be some truth in this charge, but there is something to be said on the other side also. In the first place, the difference between the performance of the two groups may not be so great as it first appears to be. For one thing, the American school year is nine months in length, whereas the European one is usually ten to ten and a half. Thus the European student who has finished a twelve-year program of study may have spent twelve more months in school than the American at the end of a similar period. Also, the two groups do not represent the same *segment* (9) of the population. A much smaller percentage completes the college-preparatory type of secondary school in Europe than completes the American high school. The European group is selected on the basis of difficult examinations, while the American group represents the average. A comparison of the European group with the top 10 percent of the American group might be a fairer comparison and doubtless would not reveal such a *discrepancy* (10) in the knowledge acquired.

15. A European educator teaching in an American university observed that although the American student is often less advanced when he enters the university, he can soon make up for it by earnest study. If he does not, he may drop out. This observer was impressed also by the seriousness of many American college students and by their achievement, particularly at the upper academic level. As one progresses toward the higher levels of university training, the differences between the American and foreign students and between the educational systems become less and less.

16. A free education for all is the American ideal. The general educational level in the United States has risen steadily. The num-

ber attending school has more than doubled during the last half-century. More than three-fourths of the population between the ages of 5 and 19 is now enrolled. After World War II there was a tremendous increase in college enrollment because many thousands of military veterans took advantage of the program of higher education that was offered them at government expense. All this has put a tremendous burden on the school facilities. In 1950 the annual *expenditure* (11) of public funds per pupil was $259, and the amount has increased every year. Even this expenditure has not solved all of the educational problems of the United States. In spite of the country's efforts to give a high quality of education to every citizen, there are inequalities from region to region because the schools are supported largely out of local funds. Not only are educators constantly experimenting to find better methods of teaching, but parents and teachers are constantly trying to improve the country's education by working for improved school facilities and for increased salaries and higher professional standards for teachers. (*2456 words*)

EXERCISES

I. Comprehension of Details

Indicate which sentence fragment best completes each of the following.

1. One of the most important problems in American education is
   a. making sure that one's child will pass the entrance examinations to a college-preparatory secondary school.
   b. providing adequately for the needs of those who wish to enter the skilled trades.
   c. interesting students in going to college.
   d. providing for the needs of those with superior academic ability and meeting the needs of the average and below-average student in the same classes.

2. Instruction in the American public high school
   a. does not vary from school to school because of the use of state courses of study and standardized achievement tests.
   b. varies somewhat from school to school depending upon the academic ability of the majority of the students.
   c. varies little from school to school because there is no difference in the educational policies of the various states.
   d. varies little from school to school because it is all aimed primarily at preparing students for college.

3. In the American public school system a student of high intellectual ability
   a. has a good opportunity of going on to graduate study in a

university, although he has attended the public schools for his entire school period.
b. has little opportunity to do graduate study in a university because he has received such poor instruction in the public high school.
c. is constantly discriminated against.
d. will never obtain admission to a university such as Harvard or Princeton.

4. The general courses offered in the first two years in an American university
   a. are often designed to round out the education of the average person rather than to appeal merely to the specialist in a field.
   b. usually have such high requirements that only the intellectually elite can successfully complete them.
   c. have such rigorous standards that students whose special abilities do not lie in that particular field will drop out.
   d. offer no challenge to the person of average ability.

5. A basic belief of the American philosophy of education is that
   a. it is more important to teach students facts than to develop their character and judgment.
   b. facts are unimportant.
   c. the true goal of education is to develop the mind and spirit.
   d. learning by doing is the most important goal of education.

6. Educators say that the main purpose of the extracurricular program is
   a. to provide students with more social life.
   b. purely recreational.
   c. to provide an opportunity to learn by doing.
   d. to fill the student's leisure time.

7. The academic achievement of an American university student
   a. is low because no academic standards are maintained.
   b. may be lower at admission than that of a European who has had the same number of years of schooling, but this difference is often made up for before the end of the university program.
   c. is always lower than that of a European student.
   d. is always low if he has gone to a public high school.

8. The extracurricular program of the American high school
   a. is completely successful in training the mind and spirit of the students who participate.
   b. must guard against placing too much emphasis on doing and not enough on learning.
   c. has little relationship to what the students study in their regular courses.
   d. emphasizes learning so much that the program is not recreational.

9. The education that one gets at a state university in the United States
   a. is always inferior to that in a small private college or in a private university because of the policy of admission.
   b. has much to offer to the student of high ability.
   c. is always better than that in a small private college or in a private university.
   d. has little to offer to the student of high ability.
10. One advantage of the American school system is that
   a. it instructs the average person but not the intellectual.
   b. its ideals are always carried out in reality.
   c. it is designed for the intellectually elite.
   d. it attempts to provide equal opportunity for everyone.

II. Skimming Exercise

Skimming helps the reader find the author's organization and thus follow the general line of his thought. You can skim to see what a paragraph deals with and how the topics of each paragraph are related to each other. Then you can read carefully to find out what is said about each point. Thus paragraph 4 states that two types of problems are to be discussed. Paragraph 5 shows how certain problems came about as a result of trying to educate everyone together.
1. What is the topic dealt with in each of paragraphs 6–12?
2. What is the function of paragraph 13?
3. What new idea is introduced in paragraph 14?
4. How many paragraphs deal with the topic stated in paragraph 14?
5. What is the function of paragraph 16?

III. Vocabulary Exercises

WORD STUDY

Complete each of the following statements with a word from the Word Study at the beginning of the selection.
1. A course of training that is particularly difficult might be described as _____.
2. If a person is one of a group that is superior in some way—in achievement or in position in the community—that group might be called _____.
3. If there is a difference between the price asked for something and the amount the purchaser pays, that difference is a _____.
4. If a person recognizes differences between two things, he may be said to _____.
5. If a person's hearing is very good, or very sharp, we say his hearing is _____.
6. If a student spends ten hours doing a reading assignment, that is a great _____ of time.

7. If a person seems to show great promise of ability to do some-thing, he shows great _____.
8. A small portion of something is called a _____.
9. If you set a value on something, you have _____ it.
10. The skill or body of information a person has been able to master in some line of work is his _____.

WORDS WITH MULTIPLE MEANINGS

Circle the letter preceding the sentence in which the italicized word is used in the same way as in the excerpt from the selection. Numbers in parentheses refer to paragraphs in the selection.

1. who will attend a university or *even* a good secondary school (1)
    1. The floor of the room was not very *even*.
    b. There are an *even* number of players on each team.
    c. There was not *even* one person in the room.
2. *Still*, there is a degree of uniformity. (2)
    a. There is *still* another solution to the problem.
    b. He is here *still*.
    c. I believe the answer is correct, but *still* I may be mistaken.
3. The examination that most European students must *take* (3)
    a. Will you *take* me with you?
    b. He *took* his time getting here.
    c. My son *took* a course in algebra last year.
4. *Yet* because of its nature (4)
    a. I don't want to disappoint my hostess. *Yet* I prefer to remain at home.
    b. The letter has not *yet* arrived.
    c. He has not left *yet*.
5. Certain problems *come about*. (5)
    a. Will you *come about* ten o'clock?
    b. How did this situation *come about*?
    c. He *came about* the payment on the loan.
6. Until they *drop* or fail the course (6)
    a. He *dropped* the paper on the floor.
    b. We *dropped* the idea and never referred to it again.
    c. I hope you will *drop* in to see me sometime.

IV. Comprehension of Grammatical Structure

Combine each of the following pairs of sentences into one by using subordinate clauses or by using verb forms or nouns as modifiers. Then check your sentence by referring to the text; numbers in parentheses refer to paragraphs where the sentence may be found. Is there more than one way in which the sentences can be combined?

1. Most European children take an examination at the age of 12 or 13. This examination determines future schooling and to a certain degree choice of a profession. (3)

2. The system does offer many opportunities to the average person. These are opportunities to develop his particular skills. (5)
3. What should the standard of performance of the "average" person at this level be? There is much debate in educational circles over this. (7)
4. One of the major problems is this question. What should the true goal of education be? (9)
5. The high school paper and the annual, or yearbook, give students training in the field of publication. This is beyond the training that they get in their regular courses in English. (11)
6. The American school system to a certain extent lives up to its ideal: This ideal is to provide equal opportunity to develop mind and spirit to the fullest possible extent. (13)
7. A European educator observed this. He was teaching in an American university. The American student is often less advanced when he enters the university. (15)

V. Comprehension of Main Ideas and Organizational Pattern

The Skimming Exercise for this selection asked you to pick out quickly the topics dealt with in certain paragraphs. This should give you an understanding of the organizational pattern so that you can more easily answer the following questions about the main ideas and how they are supported.

1. What is the central idea of the essay? Into what two parts need it be divided?
2. How is the central idea similar to that of the preceding essay?
3. What is a specific solution offered to the problem of educating everyone together?
4. What means of development (explanation, examples, facts and figures, etc.) is used in presenting this solution?
5. What method of development is used in paragraph 9? Is there any similarity between this and paragraph 13?
6. What method of development is used in explaining extracurricular activities in paragraphs 10–12?

VI. Composition

EXERCISE A

In the Reading Suggestions for the next essay it will be suggested that to aid in mastering material you read, you might turn the main points of the essay into specific questions and then read to find the answers to these questions. A question implied in this essay is: "How does the philosophy of 'equal opportunity for all' on which American education is based give rise to problems in education?" In what paragraph or paragraphs is the answer found?

1. In a short paragraph write the answer to the above question. Begin with a clear topic sentence. You might begin as follows: "The American philosophy of 'equal opportunity for all' gives rise to the problem in educaation of . . ."
2. What question is answered in paragraph 6? Formulate the question and in a short paragraph write the answer to it.
3. What question about extracurricular activities in American schools is answered in paragraphs 11 and 12? Formulate the question and write the answer.

EXERCISE B

Write an essay of three or four paragraphs on one of the following.
1. What Should Be Taught in High School?
2. The True Goal of Education
3. Faults I Find with the American Philosophy of Education
4. Aspects of American Education That Are Worth Copying
5. Differences Between the American Philosophy of Education and That of My Own Country

Essay 14

RELIGION IN AMERICA

Word Study

1. denomination /dɪnɑmɪnéʃən/
2. ritual /rítʃʊəl/
3. baptism /bǽptɪzəm/
4. repentance /rəpéntəns/
5. salvation /sælvéʃən/
6. chaplain /tʃǽplən/
7. permissiveness /pərmísɪvnəs/
8. stimulate /stímyəlet/
9. trinity /trínəti/
10. entity /éntəti/
11. affiliation /əfɪliéʃən/
12. humanitarian /hyumænətérɪən/
13. designate /dézɪgnet/

Words having to do specifically with religion:
1. *denomination* a religious group, particularly a Protestant group
2. *ritual* a set form of procedure; a ceremony followed in clubs and churches
3. *baptism* a religious ceremony by which one becomes a member of a Christian church
4. *repentance* a feeling of sorrow for doing wrong
5. *salvation* Being saved from destruction. In religion, salvation means being saved from sin.
6. *chaplain* a clergyman assigned to perform religious functions in a club or other public group

Other words that may need definition:
7. *permissiveness* condition of granting permission or allowing something
8. *stimulate* to excite to increased action
9. *trinity* Something that consists of three parts, or a group of three. In Christian theology it is the union of three divine persons — God the Father, Christ the Son, and the Holy Spirit — into the Godhead.
10. *entity* anything that exists; a being
11. *affiliation* association with a group, or act of joining a group
12. *humanitarian* A humanitarian act is an act performed for the good of people.
13. *designate* to show, point out, indicate, or set aside for a particular purpose

Reading Suggestions

The introduction to this essay tells you that three aspects of the religious life of the United States will be discussed. Read to find what these three aspects are and how they are explained.

RELIGION IN AMERICA

1. The religious life in the United States shows a diversity of practice. There are three aspects, however, that are perhaps most characteristic of the country and that most often receive comment by foreign visitors. First is the wide variety of *denominations* (1) and the attitude of *permissiveness* (7) and tolerance that exists among them. Nowhere else is there such a diversity. In 1967 there were 69,000,000 Protestants in some 200 denominations, with Protestantism accounting for roughly 56 percent of the people who are members of churches. Roman Catholics were the next largest group with 46,000,000 members. There were 5,600,000 Jews and 700,000 Eastern Orthodox Christians. Buddhists, Moslems, and Hindus were found also, but in much smaller numbers.

2. A reason for this large number of denominations can be found in the history of the country. The various national groups that settled the United States brought their own religions with them. More than twenty different Lutheran groups may be identified, many of which are separated on the basis of language. Many groups of settlers came in order to have their own particular form of religion, and a number of offshoots of European churches are represented in America. The American environment *stimulated* (8) the practice of religious independence. The historic American belief in individuality and American dislike of being regimented fostered denominationalism. Yet only two major denominations in America — Christian Science and Mormonism — are of native development.

3. Some of the differences between Protestant denominations have to do with *ritual* (2). Certain ones such as the Episcopalians and the Lutherans have a rather formal service. Other groups such as the Church of God conduct their services with much more informality and a greater display of emotion. Other denominational differences have to do with church government. Some groups such as the Methodists and Episcopalians have a rather strong central organization; within other groups such as the Congregationalists, each individual church is relatively independent. Differences of theology have to do with such things as the method and time of *baptism* (3), whether God is a *trinity* (9) or one *entity* (10), and interpretations of Biblical passages.

4. In spite of the great number of denominations, students of religious practice in the United States find that in many cases there

are no major differences in belief, and only minor ones in ritual, between many of the Protestant denominations. In the mid-twentieth century two-thirds of all church members in the United States belonged to three different churches: Roman Catholic, Baptist, and Methodist.

5. The different denominations are integrated in the pattern of American life. Society is not divided along religious lines. The church has become a social as well as a religious force in the community, but community life is not broken up into Presbyterian, Methodist, Lutheran, Roman Catholic, and Jewish groups. The churches work together in both community and religious life. They sponsor many activities such as dinners, discussion groups, parties for the young people, and so forth, and people of one denomination are welcome to attend, and often do attend, the activities sponsored by another. Participation in social groups in the community is independent of religious *affiliation* (11), and one's circle of friends will include people of a variety of denominations.

6. Until ten years ago Eastern religions did not meet with any widespread interest in the United States. However, as society has become more complex, there has been a turning toward the mystical and contemplative aspects of religion on the part of many people. Some young people study Zen Buddhism or Bahai.

7. A second important characteristic of the religious practice in the United States today is the emphasis on social problems and *humanitarian* (12) ideals rather than on the Calvinistic concern with individual sin. *Repentance* (4) and individual *salvation* (5) are stressed in the "revival" meetings which have been a feature of American religious practice, particularly in the central and southern states. Yet students of religion in America contend that in America there is not the degree of concern today with individual sin that is usually associated with Calvinism. They believe that this situation may result from the fact that the material prosperity which the Calvinist settlers to this country were able to enjoy was inconsistent with the idea that man is sinful and must suffer accordingly. They believe that American religious thinking in general has thus tended to turn more toward improving the world of here and now by doing one's duty toward one's fellow man and less toward winning salvation in the next world through repentance. Church sermons often deal with contemporary problems and the duty of right-thinking men in solving them, and churches are active in reform movements of all kinds.

8. A third characteristic of American religious practice is the separation of church and state. The government has always encouraged religion, and a religious element is present in the conduct of its affairs. Congress, for example, has an official *chaplain* (6) who opens the sessions with prayer. The motto "In God We Trust" is printed on Ameri-

can coins. Yet, because of American independence in matters of belief, there is no established state religion. Although the Congressional chaplains have always been members of Protestant denominations, they have not all been of the same denomination; and Catholics and Jews are sometimes invited to lead devotions. The twelve presidents who held office from 1890 to 1963 represented religious denominations as follows: two Methodists, two Presbyterians, two Baptists, one Unitarian, one Dutch Reformed, one Congregationalist, one Quaker, one Episcopalian, and one Roman Catholic. Members of Congress represent a variety of denominations. All religious denominations in the United States are free of any sort of state control or interference, and no religious group receives any support from the government.

9. The separation of church and state applied to church schools up to recent times. They have not received any public funds, and religious instruction is not given in the public schools. In the past it was the custom in many public schools to open the day with a prayer. In the 1960s militant groups proclaimed this a violation of the doctrine of separation of church and state. The courts upheld their objections, and prayers were banned. At the same time, church schools were agitating for public funds to help them bear the responsibility for education. These matters have been the subject of considerable controversy, and practice varies from state to state and community to community. One solution to the problem of religious instruction that many public schools have adopted is a system of released time for religious instruction. During certain *designated* (13) hours each week children are excused to go to religion classes conducted in their own individual churches. The importance of religion in American life is seen in the fact that it is considered within the province of the school to stress morals and ethics in everyday living.

10. There is a strong religious influence in American life, but it is characterized by a diversity of belief, a concern with improving conditions of present-day society, and a separation of church and state which allows freedom of worship in which this diversity can flourish. (*1162 words*)

EXERCISES

I. Comprehension of Details
Indicate whether each of the following statements is true or false by writing the letter T or F in the space provided.

_____ 1. The largest group of People in the United States formally affiliated with churches is Catholic rather than Protestant.

_____ 2. Two-thirds of all church members in the United States belong to three denominations.

_____ 3. The Lutherans are the largest denominational group in the United States.

_____ 4. Many major denominational groups are of American origin.

_____ 5. In most cases there are major differences in belief and ritual between the various Protestant groups in the United States.

_____ 6. Since the church has become a social as well as a religious force, the community is broken up into denominational groups with little relationship between them.

_____ 7. Because of the material prosperity of the country, there is a strong emphasis in American religious life on the Calvinist doctrine of individual sin.

_____ 8. Because of the separation of church and state, there is no religious emphasis in the American government.

_____ 9. Religious instruction is not given in the public schools in America.

_____ 10. Religious principles of morals and ethics play no part in the instruction of the public schools.

II. Skimming Exercise

1. The first paragraph of the essay tells you that three aspects of religious life are to be discussed, and names the first one. What is it?
2. What question is answered in paragraph 2?
3. What question is answered in paragraphs 3 and 4?
4. What question is answered in paragraph 5?
5. What questions is answered in paragraph 6?
6. What is the purpose of paragraph 7?
7. What is the purpose of paragraphs 8 and 9?
8. What different aspect of the topic is discussed in paragraph 9?

III. Vocabulary Exercises

EXERCISE A

Explain how the following pairs of words are alike in meaning or form.

1. trinity, trio
2. permissiveness, permit
3. theology, geology
4. stimulate, stimulus
5. participation, participant

EXERCISE B

Answer each of the following questions in one sentence.
1. What kind of an act is a *humanitarian* act?

2. In what way are *baptism* and a church marriage alike?
3. Is Presbyterianism a *denomination*? Is Buddhism?
4. Is *ritual* found only in churches?
5. Is a *chaplain* an entity?
6. If one *repents*, does he feel sad or happy?
7. Could a person be *prejudiced* in favor of another person or thing?

IV. Comprehension of Grammatical Structure
Combine each of the following pairs of sentences into one by use of subordination, modification, or coordination.
1. In 1967 there were 69,000,000 Protestants in some 200 denominations. Protestantism accounted for roughly 56 percent of the people who are members of churches. (1)
2. More than twenty different Lutheran groups may be identified. Many of them are separated on the basis of language. (2)
3. Only two major denominations in America are of native development. These are Christian Science and Mormonism. (2)
4. They believe this. American religious thinking in general has thus tended to turn more toward improving the world of here and now. (7)
5. Congressional chaplains have always been members of Protestant denominations. They have not all been of the same denomination. (8)

V. Comprehension of Main Ideas and Organizational Pattern
1. Check the best statement of the central or unifying idea of this essay.
   a. The religious life of the United States shows a diversity of practice.
   b. Three aspects of religious practice in the United States are most characteristic of the country and most often receive comment by foreign visitors.
   c. There is a wide variety of denominations in the United States and considerable tolerance among them.
   d. There is a strong religious influence in America, characterized by a diversity in belief.
2. What are the three main points into which the essay may be divided?
3. Find an example in the essay of a paragraph developed by each of the following three methods.
   a. Examples
   b. Statement of a condition followed by explanation of reasons for that condition
   c. Facts and figures
4. What is the most commonly used method of development in this essay?

VI. Composition

Write a short paragraph for each of the following.

1. Explain denominationalism in the United States, how it developed, and the relationship now existing among the various denominations.

2. Explain the relationship between church and state in the United States, giving examples of how it operated in government and education.

3. Give one possible explanation for the emphasis on humanitarianism in American religious practice.

Essay 15

THE CONSTITUTION: A SYMBOL FOR DEMOCRACY

Word Study

1. objectively /ɔbdʒéktɪvli/
2. disinterestedly /dɪsíntərəstədli/
3. gallantry /gǽləntri/
4. stupidity /stupídəti/
5. stimulating /stímyəletɪŋ/
6. conception /kənsépʃən/
7. elaborate /əlǽbəret/ (verb)
8. proprietary /prəpráɪətɛri/
9. profess /prəfés/
10. survive /sərváɪv/
11. revoke /rəvók/
12. envious /énvɪəs/
13. resist /riʑɪst/
14. confederation /kənfɛdəréʃən/
15. devise /dɪváɪz/
16. antagonistic /æntægɪnístɪk/
17. complicated /kámpləketəd/
18. appropriate /əpŕoprɪet/ (verb)
19. ratify /rǽtəfaɪ/
20. collectively /kəléktəvli/
21. excessive /ɛksésɪv/
22. allege /əlédʒ/
23. violation /vaɪəléʃən/
24. continuity /kɑntɪnúəti/
25. perceptive /pərséptɪv/
26. obsolete /ábsəlit/

The above words may need definition.

1. *objectively* Without prejudice, or without being ruled by feelings. If a loving mother sees the faults in her son, she is looking at him *objectively*.

2. *disinterestedly* Impartially; not influenced by personal advantage. *Disinterestedly* means almost the same thing as *objectively*. A father could not watch *disinterestedly* any competition that his daughter entered, for he would want her to win.

3. *gallantry* Acting with nobility of spirit. The nation honors troops that show *gallantry* under enemy attack.

4. *stupidity* Lack of normal intelligence. It shows *stupidity* to eat something that you know will make you sick.

5. *stimulating* Exciting. The professor's lectures were always *stimulating*.

6. *conception* A mental image or general notion. One can have little *conception* about what other planets are like.

131

7. *elaborate*   To develop in great detail (in written or spoken form). The president had plans for the organization which he *elaborated* to us at lunch.

8. *proprietary*   Held under a proprietor or owner. *Proprietary* colonies were governed not by the king but by the man who owned the territory.

9. *profess*   To declare openly. He was a man who *professed* strange religious beliefs.

10. *survive*   To remain alive. A man cannot *survive* very long without water.

11. *revoke*   To withdraw or cancel. If a person is the cause of a car accident, his license to drive may be *revoked*.

12. *envious*   Feeling discontent toward another person because of his advantages; wanting what the other person has. The younger brother is *envious* of his older brother's new car.

13. *resist*   To oppose. They *resisted* my proposal because they thought the plan would cost too much money.

14. *confederation*   A body of independent states more or less permanently united for joint action. During the American Civil War the southern states formed a *confederation*.

15. *devise*   To think out, invent, or plan. This was the best method that we could *devise*.

16. *antagonistic*   Opposed. My friend was angry and so he was *antagonistic* to everything that anyone said.

17. *complicated*   Involved; difficult to solve. The blueprints for a large building are *complicated*.

18. *appropriate*   To set aside for specific use. Congress *appropriates* money for road building. (Not to be confused with the adjective *appropriate*, which means "fitting" or "suitable.")

19. *ratify*   To give official approval to that which has been done by one's representative. The Constitution had to be *ratified* by the state governments.

10. *collectively*   As a group. The colonies worked *collectively* to write the Constitution.

21. *excessive*   Too much; more than is desirable. *Excessive* speed in automobiles causes many accidents.

22. *allege*   To assert or declare without proof. An *alleged* act is an act for which there is no proof.

23. *violation*   The breaking of a law. He has been guilty of six traffic *violations* this month.

24. *continuity*   Whole or unbroken existence. A good play or novel must have *continuity* of plot.

25. *perceptive*   Wise; able to see through a problem. *Perceptive* suggestions are ones that are the result of seeing things and situations clearly.

26. *obsolete* Out of date; no longer in use. Bows and arrows are *obsolete* in modern warfare.

Reading Suggestions
This article will show how the Constitution of the United States grew out of the early history of the country, what some of its main principles and provisions are, and who some of the most distinguished men were who helped to draw it up. After you have read the essay, you should be able to explain each of these points.

THE CONSTITUTION: A SYMBOL OF DEMOCRACY

1. A Danish student who had studied in America wrote this to his professor after returning to his home: "Strange I never knew how much I missed by not knowing the facts of American history. It is probably one of the most interesting experiences I had in America to study this. It should be compulsory for all foreign students to study, not in order to fall on their backs in admiration, but to *objectively* (1) and *disinterestedly* (2) follow the events that led to the Constitution and on from there. There are mistakes and cruelty, *gallantry* (3) and *stupidity* (4), greatness and foresight—and all this together is *stimulating* (5) to read about in a time like this when we stand face to face with a new *conception* (6) of the world."

2. Had the student *elaborated* (7), he might well have observed that the settlement of the United States, a territory which in the seventeenth century was almost unoccupied, unfolds the story of a new form of government developing gradually from the coming in of people with widely different social, religious, and political notions.

3. In the 150 years before the thirteen American colonies broke away in a war of independence against England, three distinct types of colonies developed: crown colonies, *proprietary* (8) colonies, and charter colonies.

4. The crown colonies were under the control of the king. He appointed the governor, the most important official. The governor, in turn, appointed a governor's council, which functioned partly as a group of advisers to him, partly as a supreme court, and partly as one house in the state legislature. The other house in the legislature, commonly called the House of Representatives, was elected by the voters who were white men aged twenty-one or more, who held property and *professed* (9) a religion.

5. The proprietary colonies were similar in organization to the crown colonies, except that the proprietor, or owner, took the place of the king. This arrangement existed in Pennsylvania, Delaware, and Maryland. Generally the proprietors showed a more kindly feeling toward their people than the king did toward the people in the crown colonies.

6. The charter colonies were quite different. Here a group of people were given a charter by the king to establish a new colony. Connecticut and Rhode Island were the only charter colonies to *survive* (10) as such. Massachusetts originally had been a charter colony, but its charter was seized by the king and *revoked* (11). In the charter colonies the governor was chosen either by the legislature or elected by the people. Both houses of the legislature were elected by the people. But what is most interesting is the fact that the charter establishing the form of government was written by the colonists. The king gave them this privilege in order to get them to migrate to the new world and establish colonies there. Thus in the charter colonies the colonists themselves determined what form of government they were to have. It was quite logical that they should provide a form in which they, and not the king, controlled the officials who were governing them. The people in the other colonies looked upon the charter colonists with *envious* (12) eyes.

7. After the American colonies had won their independence from England, they had a great deal of trouble in forming a workable central government. Several of the colonies claimed vast territories stretching "to the western sea," and these claims were *resisted* (13) by other colonies, chiefly by Maryland. At any rate, after the War of Independence, each former colony became a sovereign state, fully in control of its own affairs. The newly independent states were not eager to give up powers to a central government. Accordingly a loose *confederation* (14) was formed in 1781, and this government, which operated principally by committees, lasted until 1789. In the meantime, the leaders in the states recognized the weakness of the government and determined to replace it by a stronger central structure.

8. These men assembled in Philadelphia in May, 1787. With the exception of the statesman Thomas Jefferson and one or two others who were also absent, they were the leaders of the American states. All were determined to work for the common good, not for personal glory. What they accomplished was to *devise* (15) a new form of central government, although they borrowed freely from political thinkers in Europe such as Rousseau, Montesquieu, John Locke, and others. In this new form, the central government rests its authority directly on the people, not upon the existing state governments, as had been the case under the confederation. This parallel system is called "federalism," and it is worthy of note that it has persisted in the United States to the present day.

9. Framing the government took all summer. There were bitter debates, and on at least two occasions, the Constitutional Convention came close to breaking up. The interests of economic classes were pitted against each other; the interests of small and large colonies were *antagonistic* (16); the interests of colonies that had many Negro

slaves were opposed to those of colonies with few slaves. There were arguments over the control of exports and imports and the amount of authority a federal government should have over the basic rights of individuals. It is a wonder that there was any final agreement about these matters. But the convention continued, and by September the government had been hammered out.

10. The powers of government were divided into three branches: the legislative, to make policy through passing laws; the executive, to enforce such laws; and the judicial to interpret and apply them. Into this Constitution was written a *complicated* (17) system of checks to keep one branch of the government from getting so powerful that it could overrule the others. For example, the president has the right to veto laws of Congress, but these laws can be passed anyway by a two-thirds majority after his veto. Congress has the sole authority to *appropriate* (18) money for government uses. The Senate has 'the authority to approve appointments made by the President. Each branch was given power to check the operations of the others, so that no one branch could become too powerful.

11. Another problem was maintaining a proper balance between the powers of the central government and those of the governments of the individual states. The founding fathers were aware of the danger that might exist in such a vast country if lawmakers from different parts of the United States had to legislate in matters of regional concern. This problem was solved by awarding to the central government only certain limited, or enumerated, powers. The remaining powers of government, to which the term "residual powers" is ordinarily applied, were reserved to the state governments.

12. The new national government, in its Constitution, laws, and treaties, was made the "supreme law of the land." This provision established the national government on a superior legal plane to the state governments. It does not mean that the national government has power over the states; it simply means that if there is a question of conflict of power, the power belongs to the national government, not to the state.

13. One of the conditions exacted by several of the states in *ratifying* (19) the new Constitution was that there be added to it a number of amendments with the purpose of safeguarding the rights of individuals. Accordingly, ten amendments were proposed and ratified within two years of the beginning of the operation of the new government. The amendments *collectively* (20) are termed the "Bill of Rights." They contain a list of the liberties that the founding fathers believed no government could take away from any person. The more important liberties guaranteed in the Bill of Rights are freedom of religion, freedom of speech, freedom of the press, freedom to assemble peaceably, freedom to bear arms, freedom against unreasonable

search and seizure, freedom from *excessive* (21) fines or cruel and unusual punishment, and the right to a speedy, public trial by jury in cases of *alleged* (22) *violation* (23) of criminal laws. The amendments contain, of course, other freedoms too.

14. The Constitution of the United States of America went into effect in the spring of 1789. This same Constitution, with only sixteen amendments added after the Bill of Rights, remains the basic law of the United States today. The government of the United States is the oldest on the face of the earth, unbroken in its *continuity* (24) since 1789.

15. Of the distinguished body of men who met to draw up the Constitution, four deserve special mention. James Madison is often called the Father of the Constitution because of his wise and *perceptive* (25) suggestions in the Constitutional Convention. Benjamin Franklin, who was more than eighty years old as compared with Madison, who was 36, had personally observed the operation of various types of government in Europe and on several occasions urged what proved to be sensible down-to-earth suggestions. Alexander Hamilton, a brilliant young New Yorker born in the West Indies, argued in the convention for a stronger central government; yet, when he did not get it, he worked hard and effectively for ratifying the new Constitution. George Washington was the chairman of the convention. The mere fact that he had accepted the post of delegate, and later accepted the chairmanship, promised well for the success of the labors of the convention. His prestige was immense everywhere in the former colonies. He afterward became the first president under the Constitution.

16. The Constitution is brief. Its language is clear and straightforward. Although in recent years some of its provisions have been subject to differing interpretations, and amendments have been made, only a few of its provisions have become *obsolete* (26) as the nature of the society it governs changes. (*1602 words*)

EXERCISES

I. Comprehension of Details
Circle the letter preceding the sentence fragment that best completes each of the following.
  1. The original thirteen colonies in America
    a. were bound together by religious ties.
    b. all had the same kind of government before the Revolutionary War.
    c. contained no colonies that had self-government.

    d. were made up of various types of people with varied social and political beliefs.

2. In the crown colonies
    a. all men over 21 years of age could vote.
    b. the form of government was much like the form of government in the proprietary colonies.
    c. the people had no voice in making the laws.
    d. the king showed a more kindly feeling toward the people than the proprietor did in the proprietary colonies.

3. The charter colonies
    a. were envious of the crown and proprietary colonies.
    b. were allowed to select the form of government they were to live under.
    c. were the commonest type of colony.
    d. liked to have the king control the officials who governed them.

4. The making of the Constitution
    a. was speeded up because the colonies represented at the convention agreed upon all major points.
    b. occurred immediately after the colonies won their independence from England.
    c. was done by the political leaders of the thirteen colonies.
    d. was solely the product of American political thinking.

5. Under the Constitution the central government
    a. is divided into two branches.
    b. has the right to make policy in all matters of government.
    c. is weaker than that of the individual states that make up the federation.
    d. rests its authority directly upon the people and not upon state governments.

6. If there is a conflict of power between individual states and the national government,
    a. the national government has the supreme power.
    b. the remaining states decide what course of action shall be taken.
    c. the state government is supreme because it is nearer to the people.
    d. the Supreme Court decides in any given argument where justice lies.

7. The Constitution
    a. became the law of the land as soon as the convention representatives from each state had signed it.
    b. included the provision that it could not become a law of the land until five years after the Constitutional Convention.
    c. could not become the law of the land until the state governments had ratified it.

     d. was submitted to all the individual voters in the country for ratification.

8. The Bill of Rights
   a. lists the rights of the state governments that cannot be taken away by the national government.
   b. lists the rights of the national government.
   c. lists the rights which no government can take away from any individual person.
   d. was the first section of the Constitution.

9. Of the men who framed the Constitution, Benjamin Franklin
   a. was valuable because he was well acquainted with various types of European government.
   b. has been called the Father of the Constitution.
   c. was chairman of the convention.
   d. was the youngest.

10. The Constitution of the United States of America
    a. contains no provision for its own alteration, nor has it needed any alteration.
    b. has been greatly revised with changing conditions in an expanding country.
    c. has been amended thirty-two times since it was adopted.
    d. had to include the Bill of Rights before some states would ratify it.

II. Skimming Exercise

As quickly as possible, find the number of the paragraph or paragraphs which deal with each of the following.

1. Problems of central government after the colonies became independent
2. The three branches of government
3. Three types of British colonies in America
4. Four distinguished men who deserve special mention for their work in drawing up the Constitution
5. Amendments to the Constitution
6. Balance of powers between federal and state governments
7. Framing the Constitution
8. Problems in the Constitutional Convention
9. Political philosophy of the Constitution

III. Vocabulary Exercises

Here are some common words having the same root as new words you have studied in this essay. In the blanks write the similar words from the list that precedes the essay.

1. interest _____   3. property _____
2. federal _____   4. continue _____

5. collect _____   8. envy _____
6. exceed _____   9. conceive _____
7. perceive _____

IV. Comprehension of Grammatical Structure

Without looking at the selection, supply the missing words in the following paragraph.

The charter Colonies were quite _____. Here a group of people _____ given a charter by the king _____ establish a new colony. Connecticut _____ Rhode Island were the only charter colonies _____ survive as such. Massachusetts originally had been _____ charter colony, but its charter _____ seized by the king and revoked. In _____ charter colonies the governor was _____ either by the legislature or _____ by the people. But what is _____ interesting is the fact that _____ charter establishing the form _____ government was written by the _____. The king gave them this _____ in order to get them _____ migrate to the new world _____ establish colonies there. Thus in _____ charter colonies the colonists themselves determined _____ form of government they were _____ have. It was quite logical that _____ should provide a form in _____ they, and not the king, _____ the officials who were governing _____. The people in the other colonies _____ upon the charter colonists _____ envious eyes.

V. Comprehension of Main Ideas and Organizational Pattern

1. Which of the following is the best statement of the central idea of the essay?
   a. The Constitution of the United States created the first democracy in the New World.
   b. The government of the United States under the Constitution is a new form which developed gradually from roots in colonial times.
   c. The basis of the Constitution is federalism.
   d. To understand the government of the United States, one should follow the events that led to the Constitution.
2. Why does the essay begin with a description of the kinds of British colonies in North America? What is the relationship of this topic to the account of the forming of the Constitution?
3. Which of the topics in the Skimming Exercise represent the main points of the essay?
4. Here are main points developed in this essay. On another sheet of paper expand this outline by filling in sub-points (A, B, C) as needed under the main points. Also insert the topic sentence.
   I. Three types of government existed in the colonies before the American Revolution.

II. A confederation was the first form of government after the colonies won independence. (1781 – 1789)

III. The Constitution (1789), basis of today's government, was the result of many philosophies, and much debate among able men.

IV. The main points of the Constitution adopted in 1789 are as follows.

V. Sixteen amendments besides those in the Bill of Rights have been added to the Constitution to fit a changing society.

VI. Composition

EXERCISE A

Write a paragraph beginning with one of the following topic sentences.

1. I consider _____ the most important political right because . . . .
2. There were many difficulties to be settled before the United States Constitution could be adopted.
3. A small country has definite advantages in operating a democracy.
4. The most interesting American political figure to me is _____ because . . . .

EXERCISE B

Write a short composition on one of the following topics.

1. The Plan of National Government in My Country
2. Advantages of Federal Representative Government
3. A Political Problem of My Country
4. A Problem Involved in Federated World Government

Essay 16
POLITICAL PARTIES IN THE UNITED STATES

Word Study

1. sectionalism /sékʃənəlɪzm/
2. uniformity /yunɪfɔ́rmətɪ/
3. logician /lodʒíʃən/
4. lobbyist /lɑ́biɪst/
5. impressive /ɪmprésɪv/
6. diametrically /daɪəmétrɪkli/
7. heterogeneous /hétərədʒínɪəs/
8. amorphous /əmɔ́rfəs/
9. disparate /díspərət/
10. faction /fǽkʃən/
11. platform /plǽtfɔrm/
12. plank /plǽŋk/
13. dues /duz/
14. coalition /koəlíʃən/
15. stalemate /stélmet/
16. compromise /kɑmprəmaɪz/
17. tariff /térəf/
18. expel /ekspél/
19. embrace /ɛmbrés/
20. factor /fǽktər/
21. rational /rǽʃənəl/
22. collapse /kəlǽps/
23. criterion /kraɪtíriən/
24. reconcile /rékənsaɪl/
25. vast /vǽst/
26. paralysis /pərǽləsɪs/
27. defect /dífɛkt/
28. alteration /ɔltəréʃən/

Words related to words you may already know (related words are given in parentheses):

1. *sectionalism* in government, thinking that the welfare of one's own section of the country is more important than the welfare of the whole country (section)
2. *uniformity* state of being alike; having the same form, rate, manner (uniform)
3. *logician* an expert in the art of correct reasoning (logic)
4. *lobbyist* a person who works, so to speak, in the hall or lobby to try to get a legislator to vote for measures favorable to the group the lobbyist represents (lobby)
5. *impressive* forced on the memory because of the feelings that have been aroused (press, impress)
6. *diametrically* running straight through; absolutely (diameter)

Words that are often used in describing political parties and the formation of their policies:

7. *heterogeneous* political parties in the United States are *heterogeneous* (made up of unlike parts).

141

8. *amorphous*   They are *amorphous* (without definite form) collections.

9. *disparate*   They consist of *disparate* elements (parts that are not alike).

10. *faction*   Within the party are many *factions* (groups, each of which has a different aim).

11. *platform*   Each party has a *platform* (statement of beliefs).

12. *plank*   The platform of a party contains *planks* (single beliefs).

13. *dues*   An American political party does not require *dues* (money paid in order to belong) of its members.

14. *coalition*   Sometimes groups within a political party, or similar groups in two different parties, form a *coalition* (temporary union) to accomplish a particular purpose.

15. *stalemate*   Sometimes the opposing groups meet a *stalemate* (situation where it is impossible for either side to act).

16. *compromise*   In this case, often a *compromise* (a settlement in which each side gives up some demands) must be worked out.

Other words that may need definition:

17. *tariff*   a tax on goods brought into the country

18. *expel*   to remove or throw out forcibly

19. *embrace*   to clasp in the arms; to accept readily

20. *factor*   an element or part that makes a thing what it is

21. *rational*   reasonable

22. *collapse*   to break down suddenly

23. *criterion*   a standard or test by which a judgment can be formed

24. *reconcile*   to win over to friendliness; to make no longer opposed

25. *vast*   of very great size.

26. *paralysis*   a lack of ability to act or to move

27. *defect*   a lack of something necessary for completeness; an imperfection

28. *alteration*   a change; act of making something different

Reading Suggestions

The first two paragraphs of this selection explain how political parties in the United States developed. The rest of the essay explains the result of this development. Note how each paragraph develops logically out of the preceding one, and look for the transitional words that relate each paragraph to the preceding one.

POLITICAL PARTIES IN THE UNITED STATES

1. In the United States there are two major political parties, the Democratic and the Republican. The Democratic party is the older of the two, tracing its history back to the time of Andrew Jackson in the 1820s. The Republican party, which followed the Federalist party

and the Whigs, was organized in the 1850s primarily as an anti-slavery party. Since antislavery sentiment was strongest in the manufacturing area of the North and East, the Republican party logically adopted the protective *tariff* (17) and other ideas furthering the growth of manufacturing in the United States. In 1860 the Democratic party was split into two *factions* (10), the northern and the southern Democrats, each putting up its own candidate for president. While the two factions together polled more votes than did the Republican ticket, the Republicans received a total higher than that of either faction of the Democrats, and Abraham Lincoln was elected president.

2. From 1860 to the present day there have been many attempts to found new parties. Among third parties that have been able to collect *impressive* (5) vote totals have been the Populists in the 1880s, the Bull Moose Progressives of Theodore Roosevelt in 1912, and the Progressives of Robert LaFollette in 1924, and the American Party of George Wallace of Alabama in 1964 and 1968. In the past whenever a third party has had considerable appeal at the polls, one or both of the major parties in the next election has *embraced* (19) the *platform* (11) *plank* (12) accounting for its appeal, and the third party has faded away.

3. Over the years, therefore, the positions of the two major parties have been changing and adapting themselves to the currently important problems of public policy. At one time the Democratic party was considered to be a party standing up for state rights, and the Republican party a party representing the interests of business and industry. A clear-cut difference between the two parties, however, has not existed for more than half a century. If one reads the platforms of the two parties, one finds that there is very little difference between them. Each party seems to be appealing to practically every group of voters. Unlike the political parties of Europe, and unlike the Conservatives and Laborites in England, the political parties in the United States are *amorphous* (8) collections of many *disparate* (8) elements.

4. That the two parties greatly resemble each other comes about chiefly because of two *factors* (20). One is that on a national basis each political party is actually a loose association of the party organizations within the various states. The party organization in one state cannot impose its will on the party organization in any other state. Thus the nature of the Republican party in Ohio is different from the nature of the Republican party in Oregon. The second reason for the amorphous nature of political parties in the United States is that each party is more interested in winning elections than in putting across a particular policy or law. Each party is continuously seeking to find a combination of candidates and platform planks that will win elec-

tions. If one party finds that its position is considerably to the right of public opinion, it will move its position nearer to the center in order to capture more votes. If a party lies to the left, it too will try to move toward the center of public opinion. It has been aptly said that each political party is not a single party, but a collection of fifty parties which are temporarily drawn together every four years for the purpose of winning the presidency.

5. If the two major political parties are *heterogeneous* (7) groups, who pays attention to principles? The answer is that there are two groups that do so. First, there are pressure groups—special-interest organizations maintaining paid *lobbyists* (4) in the nation's capital to talk to members of Congress and endeavor to get them to vote favorably in accordance with the interests of the pressure group. There are three times as many full-time paid lobbyists in Washington, D.C., as there are members of Congress. Well-known pressure groups include the National Association of Manufacturers, the American Federation of Labor–Congress of Industrial Organizations, the American Legion, and the American Medical Association. There are hundreds of others. Every group whose interests are even remotely touched by government seems to maintain an office in Washington. The second answer to the question is that the members of Congress also pay attention to principles. In one and the same campaign, it is possible to find a candidate running on the Republican ticket in one state whose position on a number of issues is *diametrically* (6) opposed to the position of another Republican candidate running in another state. Moreover, when voting in Congress, elected congressmen pay little attention to the official position of their party. Independent voting is never punished by the party leaders.

6. Political parties in the United States are entirely free of the party discipline that characterizes political parties in Europe and Asia. It is not necessary to make an application to join the Democratic or the Republican party; there are no membership *dues* (13); party leaders cannot *expel* (18) a member. The nature of the election laws in some states, in fact, makes it possible for a voter to keep his political party affiliation secret. One could hardly expect tightly drawn party lines and rigid party control in parties that are as heterogeneous as those in America.

7. The *logician* (3) seeking a *rational* (21) party system would be quite disgusted with political parties in the United States. He would probably wonder why the system does not *collapse* (22) of its own imperfections. But the test of any social institution, of course, is how well it works. By this *criterion* (23), the American party system works very well indeed. It is able to *reconcile* (24) the considerable sectional differences and interests that exist in this *vast* (25) country. It seems to produce national *uniformity* (2) where national uniformity is desirable

and *sectionalism* (1) where sectionalism is desirable. In times of national peril, minor differences are forgotten, and the parties unite to work together for the national good. Under the two-party system, furthermore, a *stalemate* (15) is never possible after an election. One party or the other wins a majority of the national legislative body. Bargaining, *coalitions* (14), *compromises* (16), stalemates, and governmental *paralysis* (26) are never the outcome. For all its *defects* (27), the American party system endures and, for the future, shows no sign of basic *alteration* (28). (*1069 words*)

EXERCISES

I. Comprehension of Details
Circle the letter preceding the sentence fragment that best completes each of the following.
1. There are only two continuing major political parties in the United States because
   a. the people have never felt the need for more.
   b. the Constitution limits the number of parties that may be organized.
   c. the major parties continually adapt their platforms to current voter attitudes.
   d. third parties have had weak leadership.
2. The platforms of the Republican and Democratic Parties
   a. have differed little for more than half a century.
   b. differ in principle regarding state rights.
   c. differ in belief about relationship between government, business, and industry.
   d. differ today in that the Democratic Party platform appeals to the masses and the Republican Party appeals to people of wealth.
3. The purpose of the political parties is
   a. to determine policy and bring about legislation to ensure it.
   b. to find candidates and formulate platform planks to win elections.
   c. to keep voters aware of their responsibilities as citizens at election time and between elections.
   d. to keep party members thinking and acting according to party principles.
4. A congressman elected by a given political party
   a. votes as his party leader tells him.
   b. pays little attention to the official position of his party when voting on an issue.

    c. often is not a member of that party.

    d. pays no attention to the attitude or wishes of the voters who elected him when he votes on a given issue.

5. Political parties in America
    a. require application for membership before one can join.
    b. require dues of the members to pay for party expenses.
    c. can expel members.
    d. do not keep a list of members.

6. One advantage of the American party system is that
    a. it does not allow lobbying by special interests.
    b. it reduces the cost of elections.
    c. it reconciles sectional differences.
    d. it provides clear-cut choice of policy for voters.

7. In the election in which Abraham Lincoln became president
    a. the Republicans (Lincoln's party) got fewer votes than the Democrats.
    b. the Republican Party was the "old" party and the Democratic Party the "new" one.
    c. the Republican Party split on an issue for the last time.
    d. protective tariff was an issue for the last time.

8. Lobbyists in the national legislature
    a. are government workers who are paid to collect information concerning important legislation.
    b. are party workers who are paid to ensure legislation that the party favors.
    c. are paid by independent groups to influence legislation.
    d. are paid by no one but are people who volunteer their services to help promote desirable legislation.

9. Public opinion in the United States
    a. is disregarded by the politicians.
    b. determines party policy in the United States.
    c. varies so greatly from section to section that it cannot really be determined.
    d. is closely analyzed just before elections but is disregarded by politicians between elections.

II. Skimming Exercise

The general topic of paragraph 1 is the origin of the two major political parties in the United States, the Democratic and Republican. Skim the essay and be prepared to state the general topic of each of the other paragraphs.

III. Vocabulary Exercises

WORD STUDY

Underline the appropriate word in parentheses in each of the following sentences.

1. Political parties in America are made up of (disparate, uniform) groups.
2. A party platform is made up of many (factors, planks).
3. The people in a given party are (heterogeneous, amorphous).
4. A great deal of (uniformity, sectionalism) exists in each of the two big political parties in the United States.
5. Political parties in the United States do not have (dues, defects).
6. Political party membership is (heterogeneous, rational).
7. Attempted compromise often results in (paralysis, a stalemate).
8. A logician would see the (defects, collapse) of American political parties.
9. If a third party has had considerable appeal in an election, one or both of the major parties will (embrace, reconcile) the platform plank accounting for its appeal in the next election.

IDIOMATIC AND FIGURATIVE LANGUAGE

Circle the letter preceding the sentence which best illustrates the meaning of the italicized word as used in the essay. Numbers in parentheses refer to paragraphs in the essay.

1. In 1860 the Democratic party was split into two factions, the northern and the southern Democrats, each *putting up* its own candidate for president. (1)
    a. I won't *put up* with such nonsense.
    b. They *put up* some decorations for the party.
    c. Each group will *put up* some suggestions for consideration.
    d. They *put up* many objections to our proposal.
2. At one time the Democratic party was considered to be a party *standing up* for states rights. (3)
    a. You should *stand up* for what you think is right.
    b. He *stood up* well against much criticism.
    c. The audience *stood up* for the fine performance.
3. Each party is more interested in winning elections than in *putting across* a particular policy or law. (4)
    a. I hope I have *put across* the idea so that you have understood it.
    b. The workmen *put* a barrier *across* the road.
    c. We hoped to *put* our plans *across* this year.
4. If one party finds that its position is considerably to the *right* of public opinion, it will move its position nearer to the center in order to capture more votes. (4)
    a. As a conservative, his ideas are sometimes considered *right* wing.
    b. He wants to do what is *right*.
    c. We went to the *right* of the barrier.

IV. Comprehension of Grammatical Structure

In the following sentences supply the necessary structure word in each of the blanks. When you have finished, check your sentences with the selection (numbers in parentheses refer to paragraphs in the selection).

1. While the two factions together polled more votes _____ did the Republican ticket, the Republicans received a total higher than _____ of either faction of the Democrats. (1)

2. _____ the two parties greatly resemble each other comes about chiefly _____ of two factors. (4)

3. It has been aptly said _____ each political party is not a single party, but a collection of fifty parties _____ are temporarily drawn together every four years _____ the purpose _____ winning the presidency. (4)

4. Who pays attention to principles? The answer is _____ there are two groups _____ do so. (5)

5. In one and the same campaign, it is possible _____ find a candidate running on the Republican ticket in one state _____ position on a number of issues is diametrically opposed _____ the position of another Republican candidate running _____ another state. (5)

6. The nature of the election laws in some states, in fact, makes _____ possible _____ a voter _____ keep his political affiliation secret. (6)

V. Comprehension of Main Ideas and Organizational Pattern

1. This essay illustrates two types of organizational pattern. It begins with the explanation of a cause—the manner in which the two-party system in the United States grew (paragraphs 1 and 2)—and then explains how the party system operates as a result of this two-party system (paragraphs 3–7). The type of organization used in paragraphs 3–7 is called logical, for each paragraph develops logically out of the topic of the preceding one. This method of organization is often used in explanation. Note how the last five paragraphs are related to each other.

   a. Paragraph 3 tells that the two parties are similar. What is the subject of paragraph 4?

   b. What is the relationship of paragraph 5 to paragraph 4? What phrase states this relationship?

   c. Paragraph 6 develops out of the idea with which paragraph 5 ends. What idea relates the two paragraphs?

   d. The essay as a whole explains how the party system operates. How is paragraph 7 related to the purpose of the essay as a whole?

2. Within the individual paragraphs, different types of organization and development are used.

   a. Paragraph 3 begins with a statement that the parties have been changing and adapting themselves to important problems. How does the rest of the paragraph develop this idea? What method of development is used?

b. Paragraph 4 states in the opening paragraph that two factors have caused a certain condition. From the words *two factors* what do you expect the rest of this paragraph to explain? What is this method of development called?

c. Paragraph 5 begins with a question. What is the function of the rest of the paragraph?

d. Paragraph 6 begins by stating that political parties in the United States are entirely free of the party discipline that characterizes political parties in many other countries. What details tell in what way this is true? This method of development is use of particulars and details to explain a statement.

e. Paragraph 7 begins by stating the negative of the idea of the rest of the paragraph. The word *but* at the beginning of the third sentence points out the contrast and introduces the topic sentence. How is the idea in this sentence developed in the rest of the paragraph?

VI. Composition

EXERCISE A

What method of development might be used for a paragraph with each of the following topic sentences? Write one of the paragraphs.

1. There is one aspect of political party organization in my country that I would recommend be adopted by the United States.

2. If a candidate is elected to office by a given party, it is his duty to vote in all matters as his party wants him to.

3. _____ is a politician in my country who has many desirable traits.

EXERCISE B

Write a composition of about five hundred words on one of the following topics

1. Principal Beliefs of My Own Political Party
2. The Origin of the _____ Party in My Country
3. Differences Between Political Parties in My Country and Those of the United States

Essay 17

LANGUAGE: A REFLECTION OF LIFE IN THE U.S.A.

Word Study

1. bounteous /baúntiəs/
2. derogatory /dərágətɔrɪ/
3. legacy /légəsi/
4. gulch /gəltʃ/
5. gully /gɔ́li/
6. dry-run /dráɪ-rɔ́n/
7. metaphoric /mɛtəfɔ́rɪk/
8. ubiquitous /yubíkwɪtəs/
9. refuse /réfyus/
10. ingenuity /ɪndʒənúətɪ/
11. impetus /ímpətəs/
12. lexicographer /lɛksəkágrɪfər/

Note the adjective endings on these words:

1. *bounte*ous   plentiful
2. *deroga*tory   unfavorable (used to refer to a spoken or written statement)
7. *metapho*ric   having the quality of a metaphor, an implied comparison
8. *ubiquito*us   existing everywhere.

These words have noun endings:

3. *lega*cy   something left for others after a person has died, or, metaphorically, a situation has changed
10. *ingenu*ity   the ability to invent something new or find a new way of doing things
11. *impe*tus   the force to get something started
12. *lexicograph*er   a person engaged in lexicography, the making of dictionaries

Other nouns are:

4. *gulch*   a deep natural cut in the ground; a ravine
5. *gully*   a small valley made by running water
6. *dry-run*   a stream bed in which there is no water
7. *refuse*   trash, material to be thrown away

150

Reading Suggestions

As you read the selection try to determine the organizational pattern that governs it. Look for the transitional devices that help you find it.

LANGUAGE: A REFLECTION OF LIFE IN THE U.S.A.

1. It has been said that people start by speaking as they think and end by thinking as they speak, since language and culture are interestingly intertwined. People's speech does reflect their background, their activities, and the values they hold; thus we can learn much about a people by looking at their language. Let us here examine a few of the ways the language of the United States reflects the history, the way of life, and the habits of thinking of the country.

2. The fact that English is understood and spoken by all but a very small minority of the adult inhabitants of the country tells us something about the history of the U.S.A. Although the population derives from many nations, English is the language of the United States because the majority of the early European settlers on the North American continent were British. Yet while British and American English share a grammatical system in which there are only minor differences, and those largely on the spoken level, there are aspects of the vocabulary of American English which give it a characteristic flavor. Settlers from countries other than England brought the language of their homeland with them. The influences of these languages are particularly apparent in areas where large numbers of non-English speaking people have settled, but can be seen in the country as a whole. The Pennsylvania Dutch, German settlers in the Pennsylvania area, known for their *bounteous* (1) dinner tables, have contributed names of food. From them also we get the *derogatory* (2) term "dumb cluck," adapted from "kluck," a setting hen. From other German settlers we get the typically American "hamburger." Its descendants, the "cheeseburger," "beefburger," or even "fishburger," show the American delight in new coinages. Settlers from Holland have contributed "sleigh" (sled), "stoop" (porch), and "bush," meaning back country, or land that has not been cultivated. From the French explorers, or "voyageurs," we get "portage," from the fact that canoes and supplies often had to be carried from one body of water to another, and "cache," a store of supplies. The Spanish have given "rodeo," "lariat," and "sombrero" along with others as a *legacy* (3) of their ranching activities in the Southwest. Terms of African origin are found in music. "Jukebox," for example, comes from Gullah, a dialect of English spoken originally by African slaves in the South Carolina area. "Jazz," a term originating in New Orleans, is very likely of African origin. African influences on the language

are found in other areas of living, particularly in the South of the United States.

3. Although the language of the U.S.A. has shown an ability to absorb many borrowings from other languages in the 200 years of its history, these borrowings, which are mainly the result of cultural contact, seem relatively small by comparison with the new words and expressions or new uses of old words that have grown up as a result of the fact that the restless, individualistic people from all nations who have made America their home have had to adapt to new conditions. When the first settlers came to the North American continent they found physical features that were different from those of the homeland; new plants and animals were found; people engaged in new activities and developed new interests. Words and expressions for these new things had to be found. The geographical terms "creek," *gulch*, (4) *gully*, (5) and *dry-run*, (6) and the expressions "bluff," "foothill," and "continental divide" originated in America to describe features of the American landscape. Names for animals such as "chipmunk," "woodchuck," and "skunk" are adaptations of North American Indian words, as are the plant names "squash" and "hickory." These words imitate Indian sounds but use words or word parts that have other meanings in English. Expressions that come from frontier days, such as "land office business" or "stamping ground," have been extended to new situations. A "land office business" is now a term for a large number of sales, similar to the number transacted in the offices on the frontier where public lands were sold. A "stamping ground," a place where animals — perhaps buffalo — gathered, is a term for a home place, a place that one returns to frequently. There terms have taken on a metaphoric quality, a quality found also in the expression "prairie schooner," a covered wagon in which settlers crossed the country.

4. This picturesque or metaphoric quality may be seen in other expressions associated with the way of life in the United States. Terms used in travel, politics, and sports are illustrative. In a country as vast as the United States, travel has played an important role. Although the prairie schooner or covered wagon is a thing of the past, and railroads as means of carrying passengers are now giving way to automobiles and airplanes, American English retains expressions from early railroading such as "milk train," now denoting a slow method of travel, and "jerkwater," a descriptive epithet for a small unimportant town, at one time a town where the train stopped to take on water that was carried to it in buckets.

5. Among terms which grew out of American political activities are "lame duck," (someone remaining in office until the end of the term for which he is elected, although his successor has been chosen), "dark horse," (a term from horse racing to designate an unexpected

winner), and "carpetbagger," a person who moves into a community from outside and attempts to make a profit or change legislation to suit his purposes. This term grew up in the late 1860s after the War Between the States, when many Northerners moved to the South, taking with them their possessions in a bag made out of a carpet.

6. Given the American love of sports, it is not surprising that many figures of speech in the United States stem from the baseball diamond, the football field, the boxing ring, or the card table. Although originally used in sports, many of these expressions have become commonplace in other areas of living. If someone "goes to bat" for you, he helps you out of a bad situation. The businessman who has been deceived in a transaction may accuse the deceiver of "throwing me a curve ball." The executive, in assigning duties in the firm, may ask someone to "carry the ball" in a given matter. He may indicate negative results in a venture by saying, "We couldn't even get to first base," or "We were struck out before we even got started." "Hit and run," borrowed from baseball, has been applied to automobile drivers who leave the scene of an accident which they have caused. "Kickoff," the first play in a football game, has come to mean the start of anything; for instance there are kickoff breakfasts to start charity drives. A "knockout," a term in boxing meaning to knock unconscious, probably has been applied more to women as a term of flattery than it has been used in the ring. "Throw in the sponge," also from boxing, is in universal use as indication of giving up or surrendering. "He's on the ropes" also indicates a person who is almost defeated. "Give him some line," from fishing, means to let someone have his way temporarily in order to outwit him finally; "reel him in" is used in many situations to indicate victory. "To call someone's bluff" stems from poker; "I pass," "The cards were stacked against us," and "I have an ace up my sleeve" are other common expressions coming from card games.

7. National traits or habits of thinking and acting are reflected in the language. Americans have sometimes had a reputation for always being in a hurry, perhaps as a result of the fact that at one time there was much to be done in a new country and there was a sense of immediacy about doing it. In this modern age this trait may characterize people throughout the world, particularly in big cities. A reflection of it in language is the use of abbreviations. The Englishman has his "telly" (television) and his "fridge" (refrigerator) — abbreviations not commonly used in the United States. But the American puts "gas" (gasoline) in his car, goes to the "movies" (moving pictures), and drinks a "coke" (Coca-Cola). A student at an American university may study "math" (mathematics) or "trig" (trigonometry), or perhaps specialize in "soc" (sociology) or "ed psych" (educational psychology), and go to the "gym" (gymnasium)

for a "PE" (physical education) class. Perhaps the most common American abbreviation is the *ubiquitous* (8) "OK" known from Berlin to Bangkok, from Manila to Rio. Sometimes it seems to be the one term that a foreign visitor to America feels secure in using. Many sources of its origin have been suggested, the most common of which is that it is a humorous abbreviation for "all correct."

8. The informality of Americans is another trait sometimes commented on. There is a freedom in use of language. Americans may be generally less concerned with the fine distinctions between terms such as "rather than" as opposed to "instead of" or "lend" as opposed to "loan" than are their British cousins. Yet along with this informality there has been in America a glorification of the commonplace that perhaps reflects a longing for the niceties of European civilization that were not found in the rough, new world. In the past century it was customary for small towns to have an "opera house," though few ever had grand opera performed in them; the local gathering place for the consumption of alcoholic beverages was the "saloon," adapted from the French "salon," or drawing room. A liking for titles is seen in the use of terms "professor" and "doctor" not only on college campuses but in situations less appropriate as well. Occupations take on Latinized names. Thus there are "morticians," "beauticians," "cosmeticians." A *refuse* (9) collector becomes a "sanitary engineer." There is a yearning to be citified as a mark of refinement. In a society based on farming, the noon meal was the large meal of the day and was called "dinner," while the term "supper" was reserved for a lighter meal in the evening. In the cities, however, dinner was served in the evening, and it was considered countrified or "small town" to speak of dinner in the middle of the day. Though language is often informal in the U.S.A., correctness in grammatical form (as legislated by grammar books) or in pronunciation and usage (as legislated by the dictionary) has among some people been a matter of great concern, as "good English" is considered a means of moving upward in a socially mobile society.

9. Americans historically pride themselves on "Yankee *ingenuity*" (10) and the inventive quality of American English has been taken as an example. The word "Yankee" itself is reported to come from "Jan Kees," a Dutch pirate and was first applied by the English to the Dutch settlers in New York, though it somehow shifted later to refer to the English. Ingenuity is seen in the exaggeration upon which the American "tall tale" or frontier humor story depends, and in such mouth-filling terms as "gobbledygook" (nonsense), or "rapscallion" (rogue), or the somewhat out-of-date comparison "knee-high to a grasshopper" to describe a small child. More recent vivid coinages are "carhop" (a waitress at a drive-in restaurant), "rat race,"

applied to the complications of daily living, or "striptease," used in a burlesque show.

10. H. L. Mencken in his *The American Language* maximizes the inventiveness of American English. Whenever the British and Americans, he says, have created a new word, the American one is better. For an automobile he believes that "hood" is better than "bonnet," "gas" better than "petrol," and the American "billboard" is a better term for the roadside advertising device than the British "hoarding." Which term is "better" is, of course, a matter of opinion. While Americans have been linguistically inventive and have spread their language to other parts of the world, new uses of words have developed in Britain as well. Much of the present youth culture has owed its *impetus* (11) to Britain, and much of its influence on vocabulary has crossed the Atlantic in a westerly direction. In the nineteenth century Noah Webster, the American *lexicographer* (12), conceived of an American language that would be "as different from the future language of England as modern Dutch, Danish, and Swedish are from each other." This prediction has not come to pass. American and British books are read equally freely on either side of the Atlantic. Mass communication and ease of travel are breaking down differences within a language. Yet language still provides a mirror of aspects of life in the U.S.A. (*2110 words*)

EXERCISES

I. Comprehension of Details
Select the statement that most closely represents the idea expressed in the essay.
1. English is the language of the U.S.A. because
   a. the majority of the inhabitants are of British origin.
   b. all but a very small minority of the adult inhabitants of the country speak English.
   c. the majority of the early settlers on the North American continent were British.
   d. influences of other languages are particularly apparent in areas where large numbers of non-English-speaking people have settled.
2. Borrowings from other languages took place in American English primarily as a result of
   a. contacts with American Indians.
   b. contacts with other countries.
   c. the explorations of the French and Spanish in the New World.

d. the languages brought from their homelands by settlers from countries other than England.

3. Borrowings of foreign words in American English that are the result of cultural contact
   a. are relatively small compared to the number of words and expressions created to meet new conditions in a new country.
   b. are large because the restless, individualistic people from all nations who have made America their home have brought the language of their homeland.
   c. reflect the new way of life in the new land.
   d. have been primarily responsible for giving American English its distinctive flavor.

4. New words for things grew up on the American frontier because
   a. the people were imaginative.
   b. the terms they used took on a metaphoric quality.
   c. new words were needed for new things.
   d. railroading was important in a country as vast as the North American continent.

5. Terms used in politics in America
   a. sometimes have a picturesque or metaphoric quality.
   b. are largely borrowed from sports.
   c. show the important role of politics in American life.
   d. show the American love of politics.

6. An expression commonly used in politics that stems from sports is
   a. "hit and run"
   b. "go to bat"
   c. "a knockout"
   d. "carpetbagger"

7. The informality of American speech
   a. is a result of glorification of the commonplace.
   b. results in a yearning for better and finer-sounding terms to describe occupations.
   c. comes from a lack of concern for achieving social status.
   d. is accompanied by a concern for grammatical correctness.

8. The American liking for exaggeration
   a. has resulted in a glorification of the commonplace.
   b. is a source of inaccuracy or lack of correctness in American English.
   c. has had little effect in coining new words.
   d. has resulted in vivid comparisons.

9. American English
   a. is characterized by an inventiveness not found in other languages.

b. has borrowed new expressions from Britain in the later twentieth century.

c. has created the new vocabulary based on youth culture.

d. creates better terms for new things than does Britain.

10. The American language

a. is as different from the language of Britain as Noah Webster predicted it would be.

b. is becoming less like the language of Britain as new inventions create new words on the opposite sides of the Atlantic.

c. is becoming less different from the language of Britain than it was in the past.

d. is not easily understood in Britain.

II. Skimming Exercise

To get the general idea of a selection quickly one should follow the organizational pattern and get the relationship of the ideas. Find the sentences that indicate the following:

1. What sentence indicates the main topics into which the selection will be divided?
2. What sentence introduces the first main topic? What "key word" indicates this topic?
3. After discussing foreign borrowings the author indicates that a contrast with these borrowings will be made. What words point to the contrast?
4. Where does the author begin discussing words and expressions that reflect the way of life in America? What introductory words indicate this topic?
5. What is the unifying idea of paragraphs 4, 5, and 6? Is there more than one unifying idea?
6. In what paragraph does a discussion of the third main point in the introduction begin?

III. Vocabulary Exercises

WORD STUDY

What part of speech does each of the following words probably belong to? What indicates it?

1. ubiquitous*ness*
2. bount*y*
3. ubiquitous*ly*
4. ingeni*ous*
5. lexicograph*y*
6. impet*us*
7. metaphorical*ly*
8. derogatori*ly*

Use each of the above words in a sentence.

IDIOMATIC AND FIGURATIVE LANGUAGE

In paragraph 10 note the expression *come to pass*. What words could be substituted for that expression in the sentence in which it occurs?
Here are other expressions with *come*:

How has it *come about* that American English differs in many ways from the English of England?
Have you *come across* many typically American expressions?
How are you *coming along* with your study of English?

What words could be used in place of the italic expressions with *come* in the sentences in which they occur?

IV. Comprehension of Grammatical Structure

1. Note the uses of the passive form of the verb in the selection you have just read.

It has been said that people start by speaking as they think. (1)
Language and culture *are interestingly intertwined.* (1) *English is understood and spoken* by all but a very small minority. (2)
New plants and animals *were found.* (3)

2. Find at least four other examples of the use of the passive.
3. Why is the passive used so frequently?
4. Rewrite all of the passive sentences you have found and the examples above in the active voice. Is the active more effective or less? Why?

V. Comprehension of Main Ideas and Organizational Pattern

1. Complete the following outline of the selection on *Language: a Reflection of Life in the U.S.A.* Use complete sentences.

Central Idea: _____
  I. The American language reveals the nationalities of the settlers.
    A. _____
    B. _____
 II. The American language reveals the early settlers' accommodation to a new life in a new country.
    A. _____
    B. _____
    C. _____
    D. _____
III. The American language reveals the daily activities of people in the United States.
    A. _____

B. _____

C. _____

IV. _____

    A. Abbreviated words result from people being hurried.

    B. Informal words result from people being informal.

    C. The American language glorifies the commonplace because American people want to so glorify it.

    D. The creation of new words reveals Yankee ingenuity.

2. Where in this outline do the examples of metaphoric language belong? Where do the examples of the use of abbreviations go?

VI. Composition

EXERCISE A

Write a paragraph beginning with one of the following topic sentences.

1. The language of my country has been influenced by (a) groups that have settled the area, or (b) other cultures with which they have come into contact (choose one).

2. The language of _____ has added many words to my native language.

3. The vocabulary of my country illustrates _____ (name one trait).

EXERCISE B

Write a composition of three to five paragraphs on how the language of your country represents characteristic ways of thinking and acting, or various aspects of culture. Give examples.

INDEX